Be Merry

QUILTS AND PROJECTS FOR YOUR HOLIDAY HOME

MARTHA
WALKER

Be Merry

QUILTS AND PROJECTS FOR YOUR HOLIDAY HOME

By Martha Walker

Wagons West Designs
Editor: Edie McGinnis
Designer: Kelly Ludwig
Photography: Aaron T. Leimkuehler
Illustration: Lon Eric Craven
Technical Editor: Jane Miller
Production Assistance: Jo Ann Groves

Published by:
Kansas City Star Books
1729 Grand Blvd.
Kansas City, Missouri, USA 64108
All rights reserved
Copyright © 2011 The Kansas City Star Co.

First edition, first printing
ISBN: 978-1-935362-90-6
Library of Congress Control Number: 2011927825
Printed in the United States of America by Walsworth Publishing Co., Marceline, MO
To order copies, call StarInfo at (816) 234-4636 and say "Books."

PickleDish.com
The Quilter's Home Page

www.Pickledish.com

Table of Contents

Introduction

||||||||||||||||||||||||||||||||||||||||||||||||||||||

Taking something from the past, maybe a scrap of history, a memory, or perhaps an old quilt block, and translating that into a new quilt or needlework project is what I like to do best. It could be the sentiment expressed on a vintage postcard or a symbolic folk art image I see on an old fraktur that sparks the idea for a new design. Strolling through a quilt show hung with antique quilts is an unbelievable source of inspiration...the artistry of the quilters in the nineteenth century, especially, never ceases to leave me in a state of awe. Of course I can't duplicate all of those beautiful quilts I see, but sometimes I can pluck out a design element such as an appliquéd flower, a border, or a block setting to use in a creation all my own. That is what art is about - borrowing a bit from the old and making something new.

Beautiful needlework befits a beautiful design. I've included instructions for a number of hand appliqué methods that can help you achieve great results. You will also find instructions for a little known method for making tiny appliquéd circles or berries. The technique produces smooth, accurate circles with a slightly padded texture, that fools some into thinking they are stuffed (stuffed berries are sometimes found on nineteenth century appliqué masterpieces). The Holiday Hearts Quilt was appliquéd using a more primitive technique, which I describe in the project instructions, and has a charm all its own.

In *Be Merry*, you'll find projects that are decidedly Christmas and others that will fit in with your holiday décor and beyond. Deep, rich reds and greens, traditional holiday colors, figure prominently in most of the projects. Candy Cane Zig Zag is a coverlet size quilt that will go together quickly with its simple shapes for the appliqué and big setting triangles. It will go even more quickly if you machine appliqué the elements, as I did. I love hand appliqué but a quilt such as this is perfect for that time saving technique. Celebrate Christmas features more elaborate appliqué, but with just four blocks, it can be hanging on your wall in no time.

I have included two scrappy pieced quilts, Farmhouse Windmills, and Practice, which will allow you to have a great time with your scrap bag or give you a good excuse to go shopping for fabric to add to your collection. I always like to have a "take along" project on hand so I hand pieced my Practice quilt; however, rotary cutting directions are given for both quilts.

Creating a festive atmosphere during the holidays for our loved ones at home or returning home is one of the joys of Christmas. So...be merry and start stitching!

General Directions

Fabric:

I buy top quality 100% cotton fabric for my quilt making and I pre-wash and dry all of my fabrics before I use them. The light colored fabrics I merely rinse in clear hot water before drying. I wash the dark colored fabrics (red, orange, purple, green, blue, brown and black) with a product called Retayne, a color fixative.

In the fabric requirements for a project, you may see the terms "fat quarter" or "fat eighth". These are precut fabrics that quilt shops frequently sell. A fat quarter is 18" x 22" and a fat eighth is 9" x 22".

You will find patterns that ask you to make various units such as the following:

To make a half-square triangle unit:

1. Mark a diagonal line from corner to corner with a pencil on the wrong side of one light square in the size indicated for the project.

2. Pair a marked light square with a dark square of the same size. Place the right sides together with the light square on top.

3. Refer to the diagram and stitch 1/4" on both sides of the marked line as shown. Cut apart on the marked line to yield two half-square triangle units. Press each unit with the seam toward darkest fabric.

CUT →

To make a flying geese unit:

1. Mark a diagonal line from corner to corner with pencil on two squares in the size indicated for the project.

2. Place a marked square in one corner of a rectangle in the size indicated for the project, right sides together. Use the diagram as a guide for placement of marked diagonal line. Stitch on the marked line. Trim the corner, leaving a 1/4" seam allowance. Press toward the small triangle.

3. Place a second marked square on the opposite end of the unit. Stitch on the marked line. Trim and press as in Step 2, completing a flying geese unit.

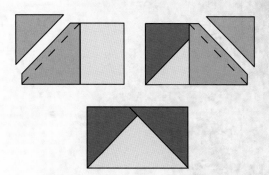

Hand Appliqué Instructions:

There are many techniques for doing appliqué. My favorite is needle turn but you should use your favorite method.

I use a #10 sharp needle and 60/2 cotton thread to match the fabric of the appliqué shape. I also have on hand an assortment of neutral silk thread that sinks right into fabric but doesn't necessarily match. Use a small slipstitch, with stitches approximately 1/8" apart. Your needle should run parallel to the edge of the appliqué shape when you take a stitch. When you bring your needle up, move the tip of the needle over just slightly to catch a few threads of the appliqué shape.

To Prepare the Shapes for Needle Turn Applique:

1. Place the appliqué template on top of the right side of the fabric and trace around the shape with a fabric marker.

2. Cut out the shape 3/16" away from the marked line.

3. Clip the concave (inward) curves, ending the clips approximately 1/16" away from marked line.

4. Baste to the background and use the needle to turn under the seam allowance, approximately 1/4" at a time. Press the seam allowance with your thumb and stitch in place. Check the stitches on the back of your work. Stitches should run parallel to your appliqué shape.

And then there are always those pesky circles that don't look quite right when they aren't perfectly round. For circles ranging in diameter from between 7/16" and 13/16", the following method will enable you to achieve perfect circles.

To draw circles for any method, I've found that a template with various sizes of circles (found in the drafting dept. of office supply or hobby stores) to be a wonderful time saving tool. It has templates for circles ranging from 1/16" to 2 1/4". Take this template to your local hardware store when you purchase your washers for the following method to help you get the exact size you need.

Washer Method for Making Circles/Berries:

Note: The templates provided in the book are for traditional appliqué methods. Refer to the finished numerical size when using the washer method.

You will need:

- ⊗ A metal washer, or washers in the appropriate size.
- ⊗ Polyester thread, any color.
- ⊗ Liquid starch.
- ⊗ Cotton swab
- ⊗ Clover mini iron
- ⊗ Metal stiletto

1. Refer to the chart below to select the appropriate size metal washer for your circle. Make a template in the size indicated. As an example, for a 1/2" finished circle appliqué, you will need a 15/32" diameter washer, and a 13/16" diameter template.

WASHER METHOD FOR MAKING CIRCLES AND BERRIES		
Size of Finished Circle	Circle Diameter for Template	Washer Diameter
7/16"	¾"	13/32"
½"	13/16"	15/32"
⅝"	1"	17/32"
¾"	1 ⅜"	23/32"
13/16"	1 ⅜"	¾"

2. Cut the appropriate amount of circles from fabric using a template.

3. Tie a strong knot at the end of your polyester thread. Select one fabric circle, and with right side up, sew a tiny running stitch around the edge of circle. Center the washer on the wrong side of your fabric circle. Draw the thread around the washer tightly (polyester thread is strong, and less likely to break than cotton).

4. With a cotton swab, dab the circle edges with

liquid starch and press firmly with a hot iron until dry.

5. Carefully loosen the gathering thread enough to remove the washer. Pull the thread again to renew your circle and press again. Clip the thread close to the appliqué.

Bias Vines and Stems:

I prepare vines and stems either using a bias tape maker or a pressing bar. If you want your straight stems to look straight, it's best not to cut them on the bias or you may get some unwanted, though unintentional, curves.

To prepare bias strips for either method, cut the appropriate width from the fabric as shown.

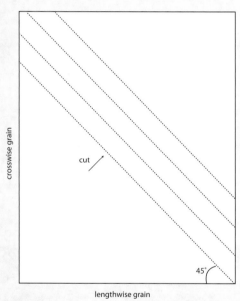

Join the strips together as shown to make longer strips.

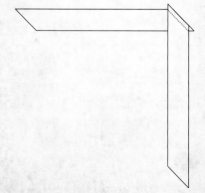

Bias Tape Maker Method:

Follow the manufacturer's directions to make bias strips. The packaging also gives directions on the how wide to cut the fabric strips needed for the width of tape you want to use.

Pressing Bar Method:

Pressing bars are made from either aluminum or no melt plastic. Follow the chart below and cut strips in the size needed for the finished vine.

1/8" bias	cut strips 3/4" wide (sew a scant 1/4" seam)
3/16" bias	cut strips 7/8" wide (sew a 1/4" seam)
1/4" bias	cut strips 1" wide (sew a 1/4" seam)
3/8" bias	cut strips 1 1/4" wide (sew a 1/4" seam)
1/2" bias	cut strips 1 1/2" wide (sew a 1/4" seam)

Fold strips in half wrong sides together. Stitch a 1/4" seam. Start the beginning of the stitch wide to make inserting pressing bar into tube easier. Insert the pressing bar into the tube, with the seam allowance centered and on top. Press the seam allowance open as you press the tube along the length of the pressing bar. Continue pressing along length of tube. When finished, trim the seam allowance close to stitching.

Skinny Stems:

For a stem 1/8" wide, I use a combination bias tape maker/needle turn technique.

1. Use a 1/4" bias tape maker to turn under the edges of a 1/2" bias strip, following the manufacturer's directions.

2. Trim away one folded edge of the seam allowance from the 1/4" bias strip.

3. Stitch the folded edge of the stem first. Needle turn the remaining raw edge of the stem. The stem will be approximately 1/8" wide.

Diagrams for the embroidery stitches used on projects in this book are below. The threads I used for each project are listed in the supply lists, however feel free to substitute alternative threads if you desire.

Back stitch

Blanket stitch

Chain stitch

Cross stitch

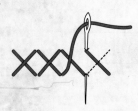

French knot

Long stitch

Outline stitch

Running stitch

Satin stitch

Whip stitch

Quilts

Candy Cane Zig Zag Quilt was hand appliquéd and machine pieced by Martha Walker, Phoenix, Arizona, and quilted by Sharon Elsberry, Maricopa, Arizona.

Candy Cane Zig Zag Quilt

QUILT SIZE: 63 1/4" X 80 1/4"

Candy canes and holly swirl about on this bold quilt with a zig zag strip setting. Dark blackish-brown and maroon prints frame the easily appliquéd blocks. The green fabric I used in the dogtooth border and some of the holly leaves is an ombré, or rainbow print which is a print in which the colors shades from dark to light to dark again. I think it adds a certain glow to the quilt.

Fabric Requirements:

- ⊗ 2 1/8 yards dark brown print 1 (includes binding)
- ⊗ 2 1/8 yards dark brown print 2
- ⊗ 5/8 yard dark brown print 3
- ⊗ 1 1/2 yards dark burgundy print 1
- ⊗ 1 1/2 yards assorted dark burgundy prints 2. Reserve two 18 1/4" pieces for setting triangles.
- ⊗ 3/4 yard golden beige print 1
- ⊗ 1 1/8 yard golden beige print 2
- ⊗ 3/4 yard green ombré print
- ⊗ 5/8 yard dark raspberry pink tone-on-tone
- ⊗ 1/2 yard assorted dark greens

Cutting Instructions:

From dark brown print 1, cut:

- ⊗ 2 - 4 1/2" x 72 3/4" strips (side borders).
- ⊗ 1 - 18 1/4" square. Cut twice diagonally to yield 4 side triangles.

From dark brown print 2, cut:

- ⊗ 2 - 4 1/2" x 63 3/4" strips (top and bottom borders).
- ⊗ 1 - 9 3/8" square. Cut once diagonally to yield two corner triangles.

- ⊗ 1 - 18 1/4" square. Cut twice diagonally to yield four side triangles.

From dark brown print 3, cut:

- ⊗ 1 - 18 1/4" square. Cut twice diagonally to yield four side triangles. You will have three triangles left over for another project.

- ⊗ 1 - 9 3/8" square. Cut once diagonally to yield two corner triangles.

From golden beige print 1, cut:

- ⊗ 24 - 6 1/2" squares (full size blocks and half blocks)

From golden beige print 2, cut:

- ⊗ 22 - 6 1/2" squares (full size blocks).
- ⊗ 1 - 9 3/4" square. Cut twice diagonally to yield 4 quarter-square triangles (half blocks).

From dark burgundy print 1, cut:

- ⊗ 1 - 18 1/4" square. Cut twice diagonally to yield four side triangles.

- ⊗ 1 - 9 3/8" square. Cut once diagonally to yield two corner triangles.

- ⊗ 56 - 2 5/8" x 4 3/4" rectangles (dogtooth border).
- ⊗ 4 - 2 5/8" squares (dogtooth border).
- ⊗ 10 - Candy canes (template A).

From assorted dark burgundy prints 2, cut:

- ⊗ 2 - 18 1/4" square. Cut twice diagonally to yield 8 side triangles. You will have one triangle left over for another project.

- ⊗ 1 - 9 3/8" square. Cut once diagonally to yield two corner triangles.

- ⊗ 12 - Candy Canes (template A).
- ⊗ 66 - Holly berries (template C).

From green ombré print, cut:

- ⊗ 112 - 2 5/8" squares (dogtooth border).
- ⊗ 13 - Holly leaves (template B).

From dark raspberry pink tone on tone, cut:

- ⊗ 24 - Candy canes A.
- ⊗ 65 - Holly berries C.

From assorted dark greens, cut:

- ⊗ 35 - Holly leaves B.

Assemble Blocks:

EACH BLOCK FINISHES TO 12"

1. Sew one 6 1/2" beige print 1 square to one 6 1/2" beige print 2 square. Press the seam allowance open. Make 2.

2. Sew Step 1 units together. Press the seam allowance open.

3. Repeat Steps 1 - 2 for a total of 11 blocks. Each block should measure 12 1/2" unfinished.

4. Sew two short sides of beige print 2 quarter-square triangles to adjacent sides of a 6 1/2" beige print 1 square to make one half block. Repeat to make a second half block.

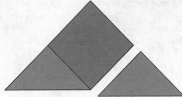

Appliqué Blocks:

Position the appliqué shapes onto the background blocks. Refer to the appliqué placement diagram. Five full size blocks will have burgundy candy canes and raspberry pink berries. Six full size blocks will have raspberry pink candy canes and burgundy berries. The half blocks will have burgundy candy canes and raspberry pink berries. Each block has one green ombré print holly leaf with assorted green holly leaves for the remaining three leaves.

Assemble Strips:

1. Sew the short side of two side triangles to opposite sides of the block. Press the seams toward the triangles. Repeat for a second unit.

2. Sew the short right side of one side triangle to one side of the block. Sew the long side of one corner triangle to the opposite side of the block. Press the seams toward the triangles. Repeat for a second unit.

3. Assemble the four block units as shown in the diagram on page 14. Press the seams open. Finish the strip by sewing the long side of two corner triangles to each end of the strip.

4. Repeat Steps 1 - 3 for a total of two strips.

5. Refer to Step 1 to make three block units.

6. Sew the short right side of one half block to the short left side of one side triangle. Repeat for a second unit.

7. Join Step 5 and Step 6 units together to make one center strip.

8. Attach Step 4 strips to the opposite sides of the Step 7 center strip to make the quilt center. Press the seams open.

Assemble Dogtooth Borders:

1. Refer to the General Directions for making flying geese units. Use the 56 - 2 5/8" x 4 3/4" rectangles and the 112 - 2 5/8" green ombré squares to make 56 flying geese units.

2. Sew 16 flying geese units together. Make two strips for the side dogtooth borders. Press the seams open.

3. Sew 12 flying geese units together. Make two strips for the top and bottom dogtooth borders. Press the seams open.

Assemble Quilt:

1. Sew two side dogtooth border strips to opposite sides of the quilt center.

2. Add a 2 5/8" burgundy square to opposite ends of each top and bottom dogtooth border strip.

3. Attach Step 2 strips to top and bottom of quilt center.

4. Sew a 4 1/2" x 72 3/4" dark brown print 1 strip to each side of the quilt.

5. Sew a 4 1/2" x 63 3/4" dark brown print 2 to the top and bottom of the quilt to complete the quilt.

6. Quilt as desired and bind with dark brown binding.

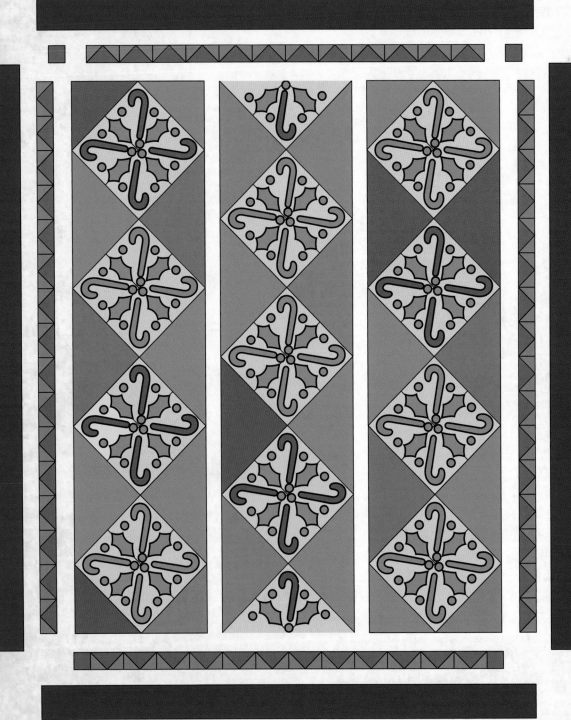

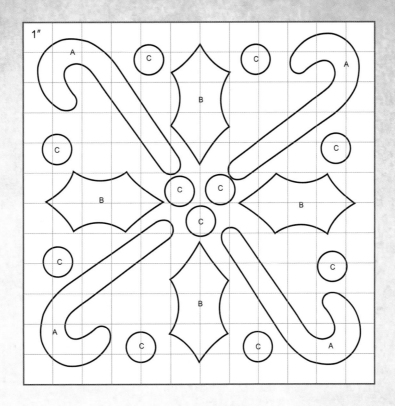

Cut 131

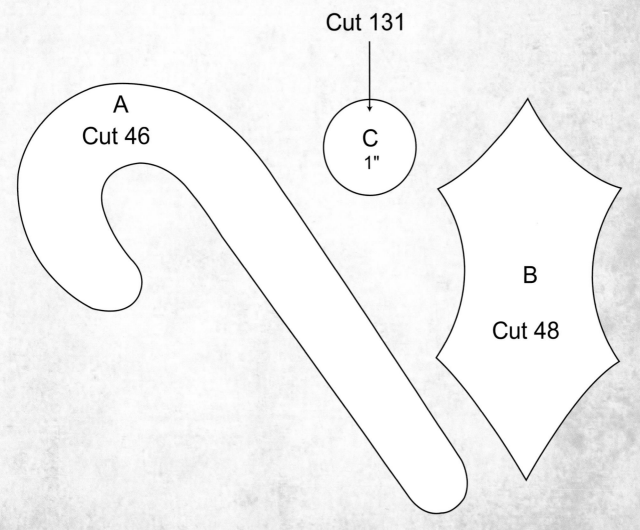

A
Cut 46

C
1"

B

Cut 48

Celebrate Christmas was hand appliquéd and quilted by Martha Walker, Phoenix, Arizona.

Celebrate Christmas Quilt

|||||||||||||||||||||||||||||||||||||||||||||||||||||||||||||||||||||||||||||||||||||

QUILT SIZE: 40" X 40"

This quilt features **four blocks** that celebrate the season with candy canes, pomegranates and red berries in swirling clusters with a floral center. The blocks are set in the classic four-block arrangement that was popular in the mid to late nineteenth century. A simple swag border finishes this graphic arrangement. I hand quilted a simple grid in the center after outline quilting the appliqué shapes, and echo quilted the outer border around the swags but there is plenty of room for more elaborate quilting designs if you choose!

Fabric Requirements:

- ⊗ 1 1/3 yards cream/beige plaid
- ⊗ 1 yard beige print
- ⊗ 1/3 yard pink
- ⊗ 1 yard red print 1 (includes binding)
- ⊗ 1/4 yard red print 2
- ⊗ 1 fat eighth dark red
- ⊗ 1 fat quarter leaf green 1
- ⊗ 1 fat quarter leaf green 2
- ⊗ 1 fat eighth dark green
- ⊗ 1 fat eighth gold

Cutting Instructions:

From cream/beige plaid, cut:

- ⊗ 2 - 14 1/2" squares (appliqué backgrounds).
- ⊗ 2 - 2 1/2" x 28 1/2" strips (side inner borders).
- ⊗ 2 - 2 1/2" x 32 1/2" strips (top and bottom inner borders).
- ⊗ 4 - 4 1/2" x 32 1/2" strips (outer borders).

From beige print, cut:

- ⊗ 2 - 14 1/2" squares (appliqué backgrounds).

- ⊗ 4 - 4 1/2" squares (corner blocks).

From pink fabric, cut:

- ⊗ 16 - Candy canes (template F).

From red print 1, cut:

- ⊗ 4 - Flowers (template C).
- ⊗ 1 - Flower (template K).
- ⊗ 16 - Swags (template M).

From red print 2, cut:

- ⊗ 16 - Pomegranates (template D).

From dark red, cut:

- ⊗ 80 - Berries (template H).

From leaf green 1, cut:

- ⊗ 16 - Leaves (template G).

Cut enough 1" bias strips to make approximately 112" of vine. Refer to the General Directions and use the pressing bar method to make 1/4" bias stems. Cut the strip into the following lengths:

- ⊗ 16 - 4 3/4" strips (berry stems).
- ⊗ 16 - 2 1/4" strips (flower stems).

From leaf green 2, cut:

- ⊗ 16 - Swags (template L).

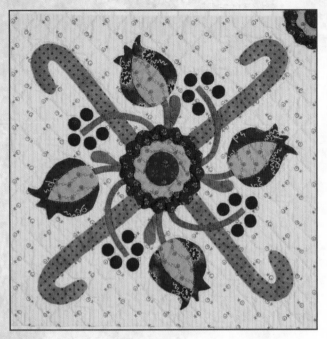

From dark green, cut:

⊗ 4 - Flowers (template A).

⊗ 1 - Flower (template I).

From gold, cut:

⊗ 16 - Pomegranates (template E).

⊗ 4 - Flowers (template B).

⊗ 1 - Flower (template J).

Appliqué Blocks:

EACH BLOCK FINISHES TO 14".

1. Prepare the appliqué pieces using your method of choice.

2. Appliqué Flower C onto Flower B.

3. Appliqué Flower B/C onto Flower A to complete the Flower appliqué. Repeat to make four Flower appliqués.

4. Appliqué Pomegranate E onto Pomegranate D to complete Pomegranate appliqué. Repeat to make 16 Pomegranate appliqués.

5. Appliqué the shapes onto each of the 14 1/2" background squares in the following order:

   A. Candy canes F

   B. Pomegranate stems and berry stems.

   C. Flowers

   D. Pomegranates

   E. Leaves G and Berries H

Assemble Quilt:

1. Sew one cream/beige plaid appliqué block to one beige print appliqué block. Repeat for a second strip.

2. Sew the two rows together to create the quilt center.

3. Appliqué Flower K onto Flower J.

4. Appliqué Flower J/K onto flower I.

5. Appliqué Flower I/J/K to the center of the quilt.

6. Sew a 2 1/2" x 28 1/2" strip to each side of the quilt center.

7. Sew a 2 1/2" x 32 1/2" strip to the top and bottom of the quilt center.

8. Attach a 4 1/2" x 32 1/2" strip to each side of the quilt.

9. Add a 4 1/2" corner square to each end of the two remaining 4 1/2" x 32 1/2" strips. Attach these two borders to the top and bottom of the quilt.

Appliqué Border:

1. Appliqué Swag L onto Swag M. Make 16.

2. Arrange four swag shapes along the seam line of each border and baste. Appliqué shapes in place.

3. Quilt as desired and bind with red binding.

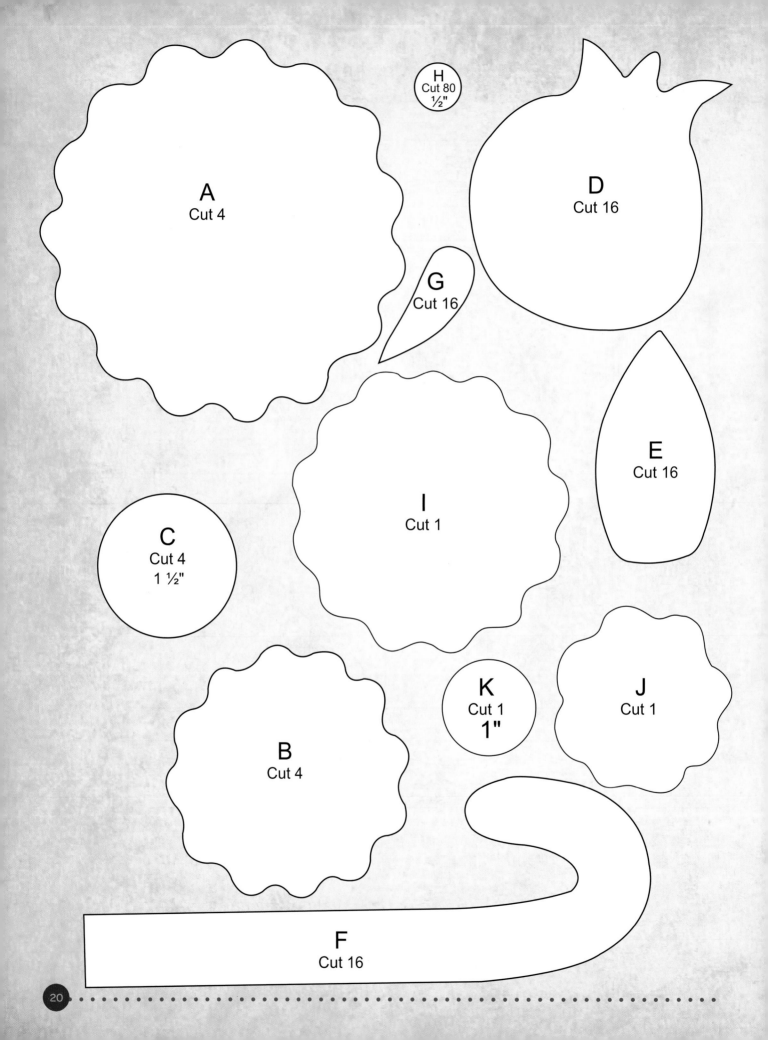

A
Cut 4

H
Cut 80
½"

D
Cut 16

G
Cut 16

E
Cut 16

I
Cut 1

C
Cut 4
1 ½"

K
Cut 1
1"

J
Cut 1

B
Cut 4

F
Cut 16

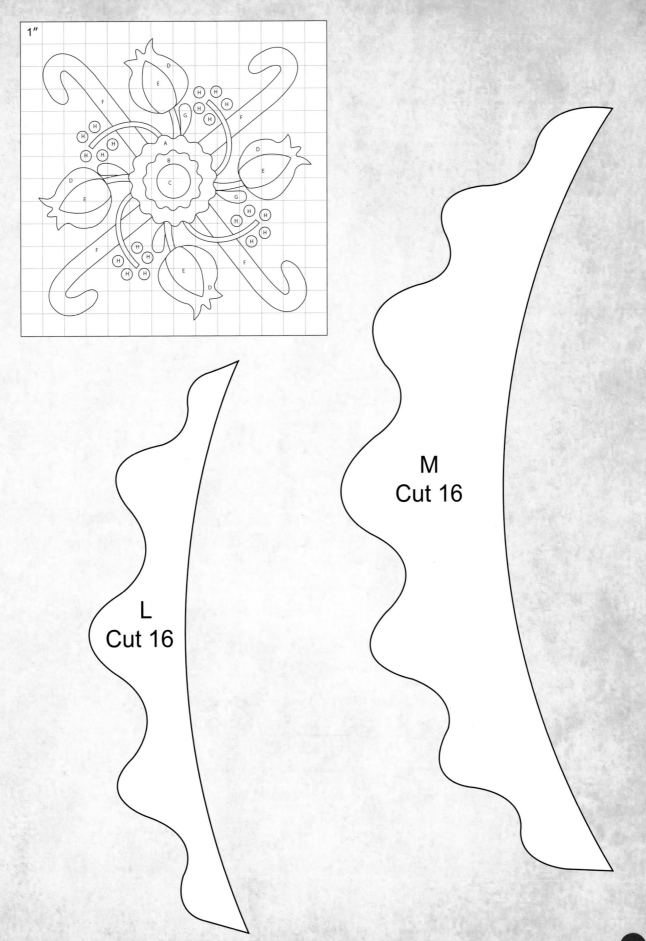

1"

M
Cut 16

L
Cut 16

Holiday Hearts Quilt was hand appliquéd and machine
pieced by Martha Walker, Phoenix, Arizona.

Holiday Hearts Quilt

|||||||||||||||||||||||||||||||||||||||||||||||||||||||||||||||||

QUILT SIZE: 58" X 58"

A vintage red and white quilt block was the inspiration for Holiday Hearts, but although the appliqué design remains the same, the colors I chose are quite different.

For Holiday Hearts, I used the same primitive method of appliqué used on the old block - raw-edge with a blanket stitch. Each piece was simply cut out without adding a seam allowance, pinned on and stitched. Because the edges of each shape are on the bias, they won't ravel, but will simply soften after being washed. The stem is the exception, which has edges turned under as it is cut on the straight of grain.

The same green print is used throughout, but there is a scrappy assortment of beige and cranberry red prints to add some interest. A trailing vine with leaves surrounds the blocks with big stars in the corners.

Fabric Requirements:

- ⊗ 2 yards beige print 1
- ⊗ 1 3/4 yard total assorted beige prints and solids
- ⊗ 1 yard total assorted cranberry red prints and solids
- ⊗ 1 1/2 yards green print

Cutting Instructions:

From beige print 1, cut:

- ⊗ 5 - 6 1/2" squares (blocks).
- ⊗ 2 - 8 1/2" x 42 1/2" strips (side borders).
- ⊗ 2 - 8 1/2" x 58 1/2" strips (top and bottom borders).

From assorted beige prints, cut:

- ⊗ 31 - 6 1/2" squares (blocks).
- ⊗ 192 - 2" squares (pieced sashing).

From assorted cranberry red prints and solids cut:

- ⊗ 16 - 2" squares (pieced sashing).
- ⊗ 96 - 2" x 3 1/2" rectangles (pieced sashing).
- ⊗ 36 - Hearts (template B).

From green print, cut:

- ⊗ 9 - Stars (template A) (blocks).
- ⊗ 72 - Leaves (template C) (blocks).
- ⊗ 4 - Stars (template D) (border).
- ⊗ 96 - Leaves (template E) (border).
- ⊗ 36 - 3/4" x 4 1/8" strips (flower stems).

Bias Vine:

(Bias Tape Maker Method) Cut enough 1" bias strips from green print that when joined together make four 60" strips (border). Use a 1/2" bias tape maker to make 1/2" bias vines.

Assemble Background Blocks:

BLOCK SIZE: 12" FINISHED

1. Sew one 6 1/2" beige print square to one 6 1/2" square of a different beige print. Press the seam open. Repeat for a second strip.

2. Sew the strips together as shown. Press the seam open. Repeat Steps 1 - 2 for a total of nine background blocks. Each block should measure 12 1/2" unfinished.

Appliqué Blocks:

1. Following the manufacturer's directions, use a 3/8" bias tape maker to turn under the edges of the 3/4" x 4 1/8" green print strips to make 36 stems.

2. Prepare all the other appliqué pieces using your method of choice.

3. Referring to the diagram for placement, appliqué the shapes onto nine 12 1/2" background squares. Attach the shapes in the following order:

   A. Stems

   B. Stars A, Hearts B

   C. Leaves C

Assemble Pieced Sashing Units:

1. Select one 2" x 3 1/2" cranberry red rectangle and two 2" beige squares. Referring to the General Directions (page 5), make one flying geese unit. Repeat for a total of 96 flying geese units. Each unit should measure 2" x 3 1/2" unfinished.

2. Join four flying geese units to make one pieced sashing unit. Press the seams open. Repeat for a total of 24 pieced sashing units.

Appliqué Borders:

1. Refer to the Border Appliqué Placement Diagram and position one 60" length of 1/2" bias vine onto one 8 1/2" x 42 1/2" beige border strip. Leave a 6" tail on each end. Baste in place, beginning and ending 2" from each end of the border. Repeat for a second side border strip. Appliqué the vines in place using your method of choice.

2. Position a 60" length of 1/2" bias vine onto one 8 1/2" x 58 1/2" beige border strip. Baste in

place. Position two Stars D over the vine ends. Appliqué the vine and stars, leaving the star free of stitching where vine ends are tucked under star. Repeat for a second border strip.

3. Position Leaves E on Step 1 and Step 2 borders and appliqué in place.

Assemble Quilt:

1. Sew four 2" cranberry red squares alternating with three pieced sashing units. Make four sashing strips.

2. Lay out the remaining pieced sashing units, appliqué blocks and sashing strips (see Quilt Assembly Diagram).

3. Join the blocks together in each row with the pieced sashing units in between. Join the block rows and sashing strips together to form the quilt center as shown in the Quilt Assembly Diagram.

4. Attach an 8 1/2" x 42 1/2" appliqué border strip to each side of quilt.

5. Attach an 8 1/2 x 58 1/2" appliqué border strip to the top and bottom of the quilt, leaving the tails of the vine free.

6. Tuck the vine tails under the corner stars and appliqué in place.

7. Quilt as desired. Bind with a pieced cranberry red print binding.

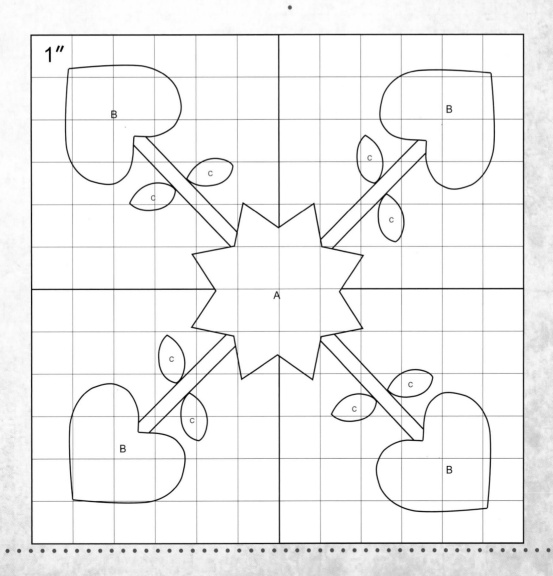

1"

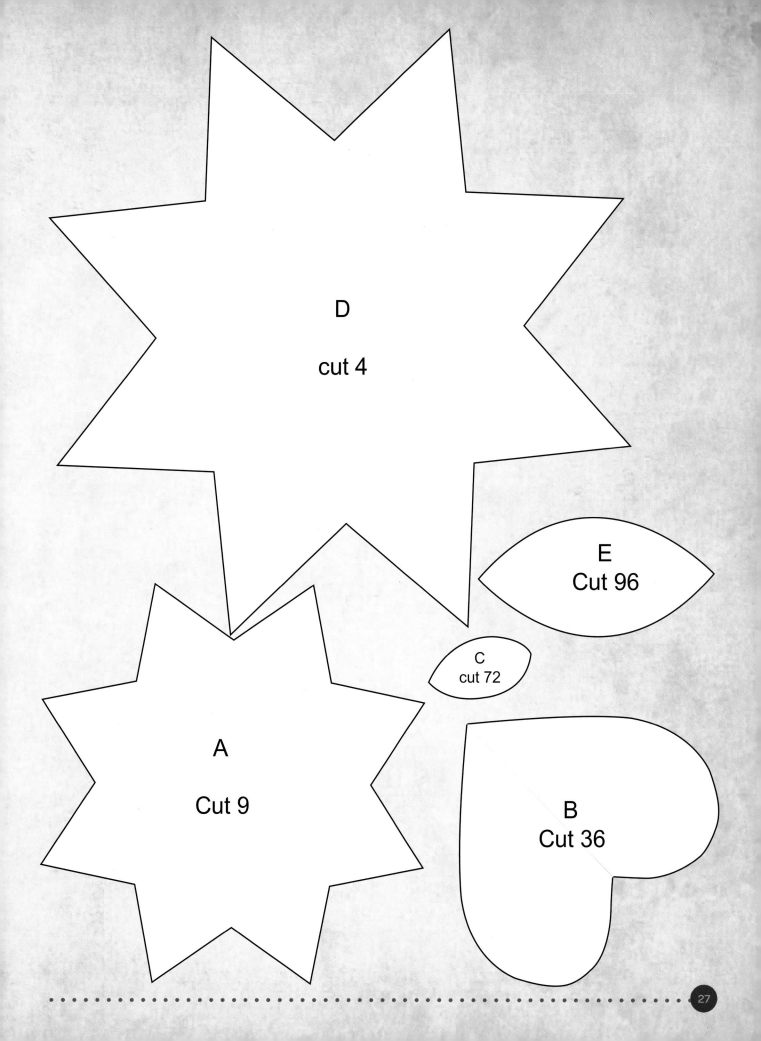

D

cut 4

E
Cut 96

C
cut 72

A

Cut 9

B
Cut 36

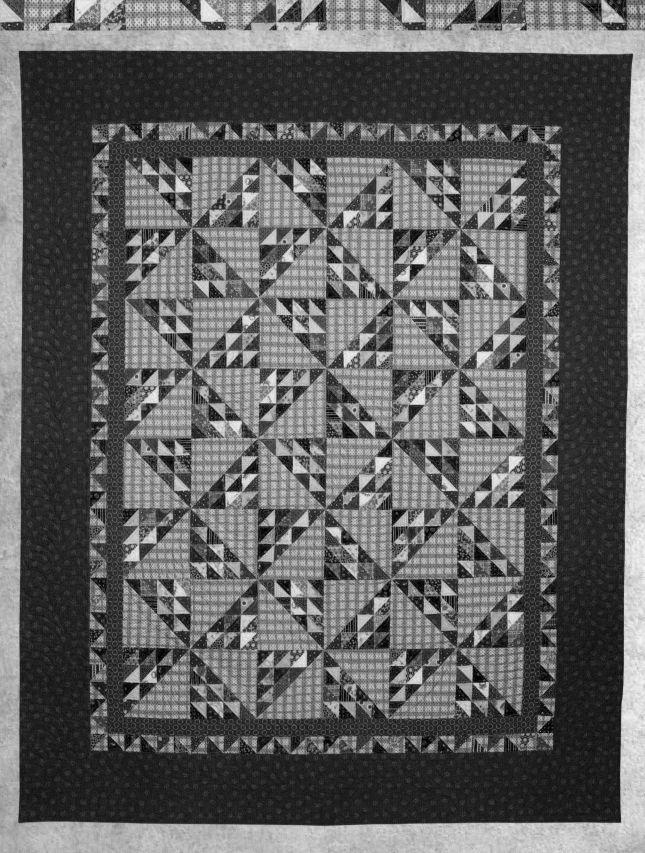

Farmhouse Windmills was machine pieced by Martha Walker, Phoenix,
Arizona, and quilted by Sharon Elsberry, Maricopa, Arizona.

Farmhouse Windmills

||||||||||||||||||||||||||||||||||||||||||||||||||||||||||||||||||||||||||||||||||||||

QUILT SIZE: 72" X 88"

The windmill played an important role in pioneering history. First made of wood and later steel, it enabled pioneers to ranch and farm land that wasn't fed water by a creek or river. The windmill is a familiar sight as you drive across our country. I can fancifully imagine people making their way back to the family homestead at Christmas and having the windmill be their first distant sight of home, peeking over the treetops or standing tall across the prairie.

The Farmhouse Windmills quilt, excepting the solid borders, is comprised entirely of large and small half-square triangles, with beige prints contrasting with deep shades of indigo, burgundy, brown and green, using mostly reproduction prints.

Fabric Requirements:

- ⊗ 2 3/4 yards maroon print 1 (includes binding)
- ⊗ 2 yards maroon print 2
- ⊗ 2 yards beige print
- ⊗ 1 fat quarter maroon print 3
- ⊗ 2 yards assorted indigo blue, green, madder red and brown dark prints
- ⊗ 1 1/4 yards assorted cream, beige and light brown prints

Cutting Instructions:

From maroon print 1, cut:

- ⊗ 4 - 8 1/2" x 72 1/2" strips (outer border).

From beige print, cut:

- ⊗ 24 - 8 7/8" squares. Cut once on the diagonal to yield 48 large triangles.

- ⊗ 62 - 2 7/8" squares (pieced inner border).

From maroon print 2, cut:

- ⊗ 2 - 2 1/2" x 64 1/2" strips (side inner border).
- ⊗ 2 - 2 1/2" x 52 1/2" strips (top and bottom inner border)

From maroon print 3, cut:

- ⊗ 24 - 2 7/8" squares. Cut once on the diagonal to yield 48 small triangles A (block centers).

From assorted indigo blue, green, madder red, and brown dark prints, cut:

- ⊗ 206 - 2 7/8" squares (blocks and inner pieced border).
- ⊗ 72 - 2 7/8" squares cut once on the diagonal to yield 144 small triangles (block centers).

From assorted cream, beige and light brown prints, cut:

⊗ 144 - 2 7/8" squares.

Assemble Blocks:

EACH BLOCK: 16" FINISHED

1. Mark 144 - 2 7/8" light print squares as described in the General Directions for making half-square triangle units (page 5).

2. Pair a 2 7/8" light square with a 2 7/8" dark print square and make a half-square triangle unit.

3. Repeat Step 2 to yield 288 triangle square units. Each unit should measure 2 1/2" unfinished.

4. Join three half-square triangle units and one small dark print triangle to form Row 1. Press the seams toward the dark triangles. Join two half-square triangle units and one small dark print triangle to form Row 2. Press the seams toward the light triangles. Join one half-square triangle unit and one small dark print triangle to form Row 3. Press the seam toward the dark triangle.

5. Referring to the diagram, sew Rows 1, 2 and 3 together. Attach one maroon small triangle A to make a pieced triangle unit. Press the seams open.

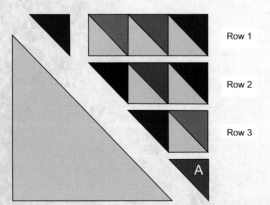

Row 1

Row 2

Row 3

A

6. Join one large beige print triangle to a pieced triangle unit. Press the seam allowance toward the beige print triangle.

7. Repeat Steps 4 - 6 to make 48 sail blocks. Each block should measure 8 1/2" unfinished.

8. Sew together two sail blocks, matching the maroon triangles as shown. Repeat for a second strip. Join the strips together to make a windmill block.

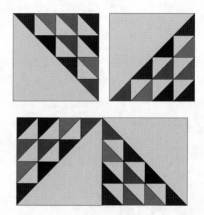

9. Repeat Step 8 to make 12 windmill blocks. Each block should measure 16 1/2".

Assemble Pieced Borders:

1. Mark 62 - 2 7/8" beige print squares as described in the General Directions for making half-square triangle units.

2. Pair a beige print square with a 2 7/8" dark print square to make a half-square triangle unit. Make 124.

3. Select two half-square triangle units and sew together as shown. Make 34.

4. Join 17 Step 3 units as shown to make one side border strip. Repeat for a second pieced side border strip.

5. Select two triangle squares and sew together as shown.

Repeat for a total of 28 units.

6. Join 14 Step 5 units as shown to make one pieced top border strip. Repeat for the bottom border strip.

Assemble Quilt:

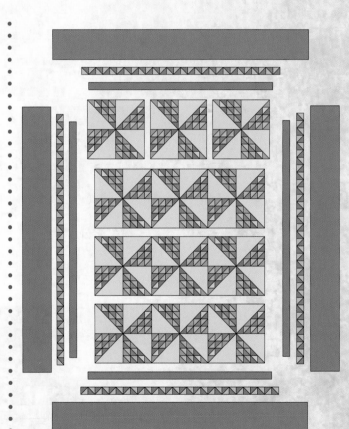

1. Lay out the blocks in rows of three as shown on the Quilt Assembly Diagram. Sew the blocks together.

2. Join the rows to create the quilt center.

3. Sew a 2 1/2" x 64 1/2" maroon strip to each side of the quilt center.

4. Sew a 2 1/2" x 52 1/2" maroon strip to the top and one to the bottom of quilt to complete the inner maroon border.

5. Attach a pieced side border strip to either side of the quilt as shown.

6. Add a pieced top and bottom border strip to top and one to the bottom of the quilt as shown to complete the pieced border.

7. Sew an 8 1/2" x 72 1/2" maroon strip to each side of the quilt.

8. Add an 8 1/2" x 72 1/2" maroon strip to the top and bottom of the quilt to complete the outer border.

9. Quilt as desired and bind with maroon binding.

Practice was hand pieced and quilted by Martha Walker, Phoenix, Arizona.

Practice

|||||||||||||||||||||||||||||

FINISHED SIZE: 34" X 34"

many of the antique quilts that attract me the most are humble quilts made from simple shapes, especially squares. "Practice" was inspired by just such a quilt, a small doll quilt made entirely of four-patches.

In the nineteenth century and early twentieth century, it was important for a young girl to learn sewing skills. Small patchwork blocks were the perfect vehicle for learning to stitch pieces of fabric together with a running stitch. Typically the young beginner stitched four-patch and nine-patch patterns. The blocks were sometimes sewn together to make small doll quilts. I can imagine a young girl making stacks of blocks to pass away the time during the long winter months.

I selected new fabrics that have a timeworn and faded appearance and added a few vintage c. 1890-1910 fabrics just for fun. Practice is composed almost entirely of four-patch blocks, my rendition of a young girl's quilt that made use of all of those practice blocks!

Fabric Requirements:

- ⊗ 1 yard medium brown print (includes binding)
- ⊗ 1 fat quarter cream solid homespun 1/2 yard assorted double pink, brown, and red prints
- ⊗ 1 yard assorted light brown, light pink and shirting prints

Cutting Instructions:

From medium brown print, cut:

- ⊗ 2 - 2 1/2" x 20 1/2" strips (side inner border).
- ⊗ 2 - 2 1/2" x 24 1/2" strips (top and bottom inner border).
- ⊗ 2 - 1 1/2" x 32 1/2" strips (side outer border).
- ⊗ 2 - 1 1/2" x 34 1/2" strips (top and bottom outer border).

From cream solid homespun, cut:

- ⊗ 20 - 2 1/2" squares (blocks).

From assorted double pink, brown, and red prints, cut:

- ⊗ 238 - 1 1/2" squares (blocks and pieced border).

From assorted light brown, light pink and shirting prints cut:

- ⊗ 12 - 1 1/2" x 6 1/2" rectangles (pieced inner border).
- ⊗ 56 - 2 1/2" squares (pieced outer border).
- ⊗ 234 - 1 1/2" squares (all blocks).

Assemble Four-Patch Blocks

1. Sew one 1 1/2" dark print square to one 1 1/2" light print square. Press the seam allowance toward the dark square. Repeat for a total of two strips.

2. Sew the strips together as shown. Repeat Steps 1 - 2 to make 117 four-patch blocks. The blocks should measure 2 1/2" unfinished.

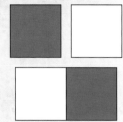

Assemble Nine-Patch Blocks:

1. Sew two four-patch blocks to opposite sides of one 2 1/2" solid homespun square. Repeat for a total of two strips. Attach two 2 1/2" solid homespun squares to opposite sides of one four-patch block. Join these three strips as shown.

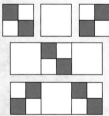

2. Repeat Step 1 for a total of 5 nine-patch blocks. Each block should measure 6 1/2" unfinished.

Assemble Thirty-Six Patch Blocks:

1. Referring to the diagram below, lay out nine four-patch blocks in three rows of three blocks each. Sew together the pieces in each row. Join the rows to make a thirty-six patch block.

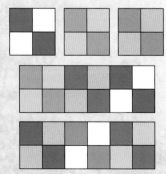

Repeat Step 1 for a total of 4 thirty-six patch blocks. Each block should measure 6 1/2" unfinished.

Assemble Double Four-Patch Blocks:

1. Sew one four-patch block to one 2 1/2" light print square. Repeat for a second strip. Join the strips together to form one double four-patch block as shown.

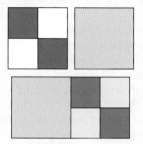

2. Repeat Step 1 for a total of 28 double four-patch blocks. Blocks should measure 4 1/2" unfinished.

Assemble Pieced Inner Borders:

1. Lay out three 1 1/2" x 6 1/2" rectangles. Sew together to make one pieced inner border strip. Repeat for a total of four pieced inner border strips.

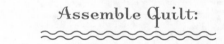

Assemble Quilt:

1. Lay out nine-patch blocks and thirty-six patch blocks in rows, referring to the Quilt Assembly Diagram. Sew the blocks together.

2. Join rows together to form the quilt center.

3. Attach two pieced inner border strips to each side of the quilt center.

4. Add two 1 1/2" dark print squares to opposite ends of the remaining pieced inner border strips. Attach these two borders to the top and bottom of the quilt.

5. Sew a 2 1/2" x 20 1/2" medium brown strip to each side of the quilt.

6. Attach a 2 1/2" x 24 1/2" medium brown strip to

the top and bottom of the quilt.

7. Sew six double four-patch blocks together as shown to make one side pieced border strip. Repeat for a second strip.

8. Attach a side pieced border strip to each side of quilt.

9. Sew eight double four-patch blocks together as shown to make the top pieced border strip.

Repeat to make the bottom pieced border strip.

10. Attach the Step 9 strips to the top and bottom of the quilt.

11. Sew the 1 1/2" x 32 1/2" medium brown strips to each side of the quilt.

12. Add the 1 1/2" x 34 1/2" medium brown strips to the top and bottom of the quilt.

13. Quilt as desired and bind with medium brown binding.

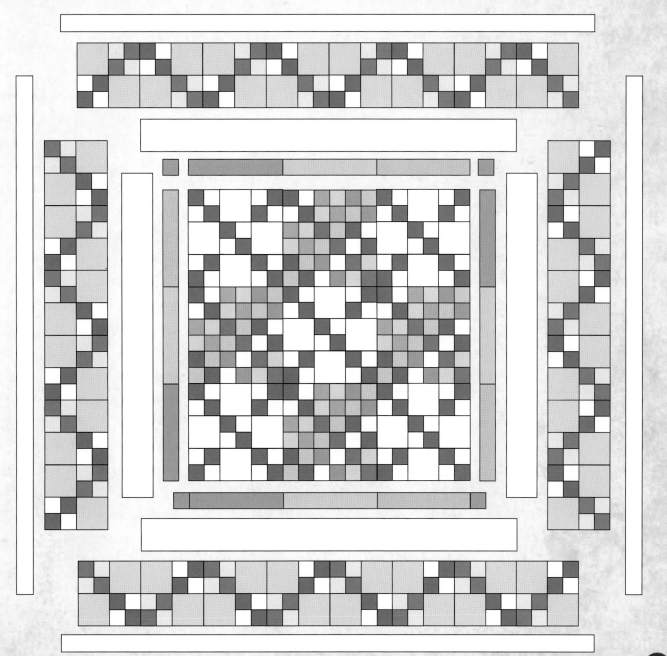

Antique Hearts was hand appliquéd, machine pieced and
quilted by Martha Walker, Phoenix, Arizona.

Antique Hearts

||||||||||||||||||||||||||||||||||||||||||||||||

QUILT SIZE: 42" X 42" FINISHED

The image of a red and white block on a nineteenth century album quilt was the genesis of this little quilt. Each block features a different set of red and beige print fabrics for a scrappy monochromatic quilt.

Fabric Requirements:

⊗ 9 fat eighths assorted light prints

⊗ 9 fat eighths assorted red prints

⊗ 1 yard black print (includes binding).

⊗ 1 1/2 yards red print

Cutting Instructions:

From assorted light prints cut:

⊗ 9 - 6 1/2" squares, 1 square from each print (blocks).

⊗ 90 - 2 3/8" squares, 10 squares from each print (blocks).

From assorted red prints cut:

⊗ 90 - 2 3/8" squares, 10 squares from each print (blocks).

⊗ 36 - Hearts A, four from each print (blocks).

From black print cut:

⊗ 2 - 1 1/2" x 27 1/2" strips (inner side borders).

⊗ 2 - 1 1/2" x 29 1/2" strips (inner top and bottom borders).

From red print cut:

⊗ 2 - 7" x 29 1/2" strips (outer side borders).

⊗ 2 - 7" x 42 1/2" strips (outer top and bottom borders).

Appliqué and Assemble Blocks:

EACH BLOCK: 9" FINISHED

1. Prepare the heart appliqués using your method of choice. Appliqué the hearts to the background square as shown.

2. Select 10 - 2 3/8" light print squares to match a 6 1/2" background square, and 10 - 2 3/8" red print squares to match the heart appliqués. Refer to the General Directions to make 20 half-square triangle units.

3. Join four half-square triangle units to make one side strip as shown. Press the seams open.

4. Join four half-square triangle units to make a second side strip as shown. Press the seams open.

5. Attach the strips to opposite sides of the appliqué center square. Press the seams toward the center square.

6. Join six half-square triangle units to make the top strip as shown. Press the seams open.

7. Join six half-square triangle units to make the bottom strip as shown. Press the seams open.

8. Attach the top and bottom strips to the remaining edges of the center unit. Press the seams toward the center square.

9. Repeat Steps 1 - 8 to make a total of nine blocks. Each block should measure 9 1/2" unfinished.

Assemble Quilt:

1. Sew three blocks together to form a row. Press the seams open. Make three rows.

2. Join the rows together to create the quilt center. Press the seams open.

3. Sew a 1 1/2" x 27 1/2" black strip to each side of quilt center. Press the seams toward the black strip.

4. Attach the 1 1/2" x 29 1/2" black strips to top and bottom of the quilt to complete the inner border. Press the seams towards the black strip.

5. Sew the 7" x 29 1/2" red outer border strips to each side of the quilt. Press the seams toward the red border.

6. Add the 7" x 42 1/2" red outer border strips to the top and bottom edges to complete the quilt. Press the seams toward the red border.

7. Quilt as desired and bind with black binding.

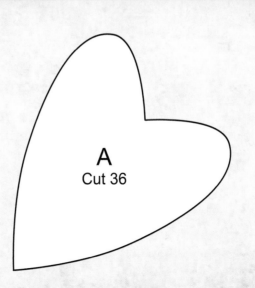

A
Cut 36

Bricks and Boughs Table Runner was hand appliquéd, machine pieced and quilted by Martha Walker, Phoenix, Arizona.

Bricks and Boughs Table Runner

SIZE: 24" X 48" FINISHED

Adorn your table with fabric boughs, pineapples and berries. The pieced brick center serves as a backdrop for your holiday centerpiece. Choose fabrics for the center that are close in value so they blend together.

Fabric Requirements:

- ⊗ 1 1/2 yards mottled beige fabric
- ⊗ 1 yard total assorted dark cranberry red, dark blue-green, and dark brown prints, solids, and plaids
- ⊗ 1/3 yard cranberry red stripe for binding
- ⊗ 1 fat quarter very dark blue-green plaid
- ⊗ 1 fat quarter dark gray-green
- ⊗ 1 fat eighth blue-green check
- ⊗ 10" square orange-yellow print
- ⊗ 2 - 10" squares two different red prints
- ⊗ 1 fat eighth red solid
- ⊗ Scraps assorted gold prints

Cutting Instructions:

From mottled beige fabric, cut:

- ⊗ 2 - 8" x 48 1/2" strips (appliqué backgrounds).

From assorted dark cranberry red, dark blue green and dark brown fabrics, cut:

- ⊗ 140 - 1 1/2" x 3 1/2" rectangles (pieced center).
- ⊗ 8 - 1 1/2" x 2" rectangles (pieced center).

From assorted dark blue-green fabrics, cut:

- ⊗ 4 - Leaves (reverse 2) (template A).
- ⊗ 4 - Leaves (reverse 2) (template B).
- ⊗ 4 - Leaves (reverse 2) (template C).
- ⊗ 4 - Leaves (reverse 2) (template D).
- ⊗ 4 - Leaves (reverse 2) (template E).

From assorted dark brown fabrics, cut:

- ⊗ 1 - 7/8" x 12" strip. Use the pressing bar method to make a 3/16" tube. Cut the tube into 8 - 1 1/2" lengths for the bird's legs.

From very dark blue-green plaid, cut:

- ⊗ 1" bias strips to make 4 - 24" lengths of 1/4" bias vines using the pressing bar method for the main vine.

From dark gray/green, cut:

- ⊗ 1" bias strips to make 114" of 1/4 bias vine for the berry stems. Use the pressing bar method.
- ⊗ 1 - 7/8" x 7" bias strip. Use the pressing bar method to make a 3/16" bias tube. Cut the tube into 4 - 1 3/4" pieces for the stems held by the birds.

From the blue-green check, cut:

- ⊗ 2 - Pineapple leaves (template F).

From orange-yellow print, cut:

⊗ 2 - Pineapples (template G).

From red prints, cut:

⊗ 4 - Birds (reverse 2) (template H).

From red solid, cut:

⊗ 52 - Berries (template L).

⊗ 4 - Berries (template M).

From assorted gold prints, cut:

⊗ 4 - Wings I (reverse 2) (template I).

⊗ 4 - Collars (reverse 2) (template J).

⊗ 4 - Birds eyes (template K).

Assemble Pieced Center:

1. To make row A, sew together 16 - 1 1/2" x 3 1/2" rectangles. Make 5.

2. To make row B, sew together 15 - 1 1/2" x 3 1/2" rectangles. Attach a 1 1/2" x 2" rectangle to opposite ends of each strip. Make 4.

3. Sew rows A and B together in an A B A B A B A B A pattern.

Appliqué Panels:

1. Cut strips from the 1/4" dark gray-green bias tubing to the size needed for each berry stem. Refer to the appliqué placement diagram on page 46.

2. Baste the berry stems in place onto one 8" x 48 1/2" beige strip.

3. Baste two 24" lengths of 1/4" blue-green plaid bias vines in place. Appliqué the berry stems and main vine in place.

4. Appliqué the remaining pieces in the following order:

   A. Pineapple leaves F.

   B. Pineapple G.

   C. Birds' eye K and Birds' collars J to Birds H to create Bird Bodies.

   D. Birds' legs.

   E. Bird Bodies.

   F. Birds' wings I.

   G. Leaves A, B, C, D and E.

   H. Berries L.

   I. Stems in birds' beak.

   J. Berries M.

5. Repeat Steps 1 - 4 to make a second appliqué panel.

6. Attach the two appliqué panels to opposite sides of the pieced center.

7. Quilt as desired. Bind with cranberry red binding.

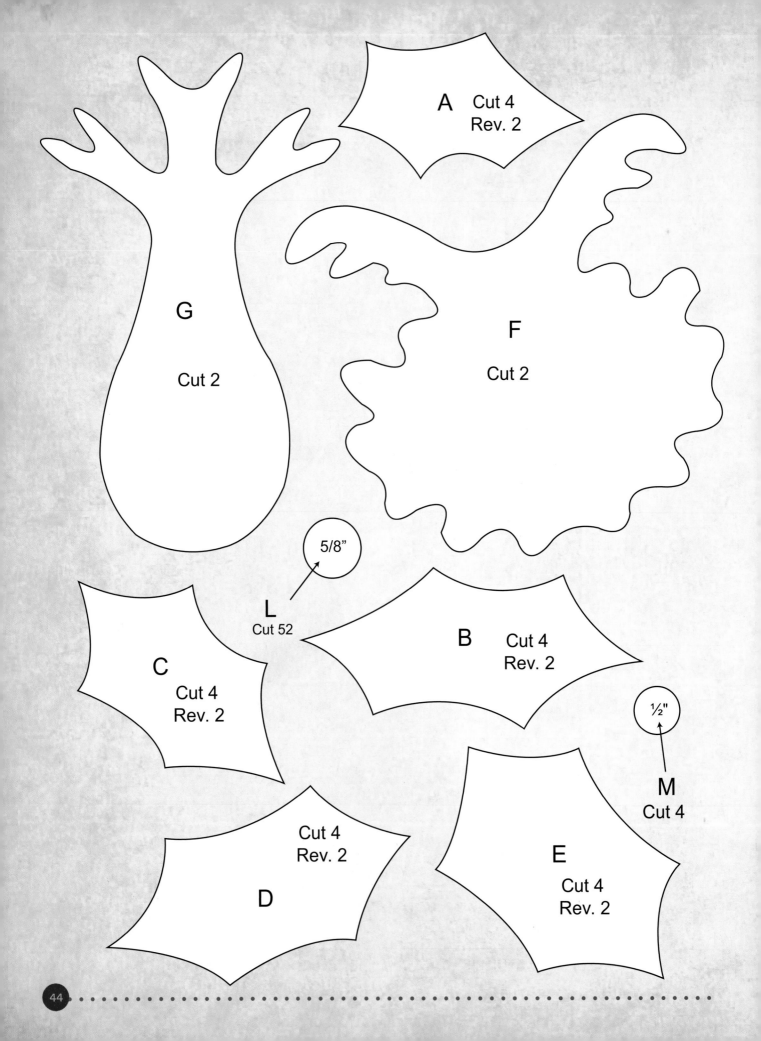

A Cut 4 Rev. 2

G Cut 2

F Cut 2

L Cut 52

5/8"

C Cut 4 Rev. 2

B Cut 4 Rev. 2

M Cut 4

1/2"

Cut 4 Rev. 2

D

E Cut 4 Rev. 2

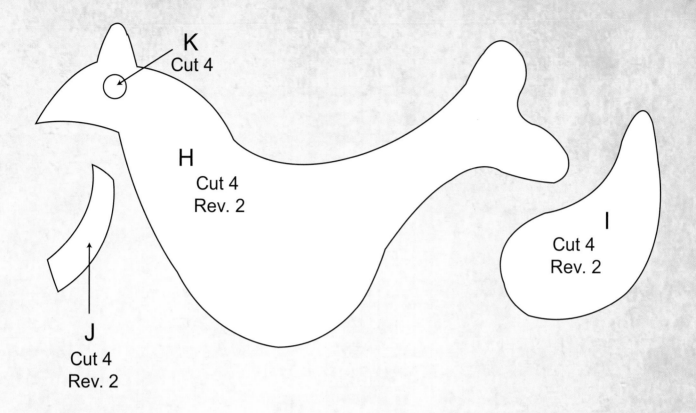

K
Cut 4

H
Cut 4
Rev. 2

I
Cut 4
Rev. 2

J
Cut 4
Rev. 2

Projects

BLESSINGS

Be Merry Journal Cover was made by
Martha Walker, Phoenix, Arizona.

Be Merry Journal Cover

||||||||||||||||||||||||||||||||||||||||||||||||||||||||||||||||||||||||||||||||||||||||||||||||||||

FITS A STANDARD 7 1/2" X 9 3/4" COMPOSITION BOOK WITH A 3/8" SPINE.

This merry little project was so much fun to make! A basketful of buds and berries, with a cheerful little note attached adorn the Be Merry Journal Cover. Make several so you'll have gifts on hand for special friends.

I used reproduction fabrics. Small prints work best for these little appliqué pieces.

Fabric Requirements:

- ⊗ 1 fat quarter light print
- ⊗ 1 fat quarter light weight beige flannel
- ⊗ 1 fat quarter red print 1
- ⊗ 1 fat eighth red tone-on-tone
- ⊗ 4" x 6" rectangle medium beige print
- ⊗ 4" x 6" rectangle beige stripe
- ⊗ 3" x 5" rectangle green tone-on-tone 1
- ⊗ 4" square green tone-on-tone 2
- ⊗ 2" square green and red print
- ⊗ 2 1/2" square red print 2
- ⊗ 5 1/2" square tea-dyed muslin
- ⊗ Scrap of light brown

Other Supplies:

- ⊗ DMC embroidery floss 3371
- ⊗ 4" diameter embroidery hoop
- ⊗ Embroidery needle
- ⊗ 40 wt. black cotton quilting thread
- ⊗ 16" length of 1/2" tea-dyed cotton twill tape

Cutting Instructions:

From light print, cut:
- ⊗ 1 - 9 1/2" x 10 1/2" rectangle (front cover).

From beige flannel, cut:
- ⊗ 1 - 10 1/2" x 16 1/4" rectangle (cover lining).

From red print 1, cut:
- ⊗ 1 - 7 3/4" x 10 1/2" rectangle (back cover).
- ⊗ 2 - 3" x 10 1/2" strips (side facings).
- ⊗ 2 - 1 1/2" x 13" strips (top and bottom facings).
- ⊗ 1 - Basket foot (template M).
- ⊗ 2 - Hearts (reverse 1) (template O).

From red tone-on-tone, cut:
- ⊗ 2 - Dogtooth borders (template I).
- ⊗ 1 - Dogtooth border (template J).
- ⊗ 1 - Dogtooth border (template K).

Note: Do not add a seam allowance to pieces I, J, and K where indicated on the templates.

- ⊗ 22 - Berries (template P).

From medium beige print, cut:
- ⊗ 1 - Basket (template L).

From beige stripe, cut:

- ⊗ 1 - Basket handle (template N).

From green tone-on-tone 1, cut:

- ⊗ 1 - 1/2" x 4 1/4" bias strip (berry stem).
- ⊗ 1 - 1/2" x 4 1/2" bias strip (berry stem).
- ⊗ 1 - 1/2" x 5" bias strip (berry stem).
- ⊗ 1 - Leaf (template F).
- ⊗ 1 - Leaf (template G).

From green tone-on-tone 2, cut:

- ⊗ 1 - Flower (template A).
- ⊗ 1 - Flower (template B).
- ⊗ 1 - Flower (template C).
- ⊗ 1 - Leaf (template D).
- ⊗ 1 - Leaf (template E).
- ⊗ 1 - Leaf (template H).

From green and red print, cut:

- ⊗ 2 - Hearts (reverse 1) (template O).

From red print 2, cut:

- ⊗ 1 - Flower (template AA).
- ⊗ 1 - Flower (template BB).
- ⊗ 1 - Flower (template CC).

From light brown, cut:

- ⊗ 1 - Tag circle (template R).

From twill tape, cut:

- ⊗ 2 - 8" lengths.

Embroider Tag:

1. Transfer "Be Merry" lettering onto the center of the 5 1/2" muslin square.

2. Put the fabric square in a hoop and backstitch the lettering using 3 strands of DMC 3371 embroidery floss.

3. Trace Tag Q onto the fabric square to complete the tag appliqué piece.

Appliqué Shapes:

1. Place all four dogtooth border shapes onto the 9 1/2" x 10 1/2" light print rectangle to fit. Baste. Appliqué the outer points and sides of the dogtooth pieces.

2. Prepare the green bias strips for stems, referring to "Skinny Stems" directions.

3. Appliqué the shapes in the following order:

   A. Basket handle N.

   B. Berry stems.

   C. Basket L.

   D. Basket foot M.

   E. Leaves D, E, F, G, and H.

   F. Tag Q.

   G. Tag circle R.

   H. Flowers AA, BB, and CC.

   I. Flowers A, B, and C.

   J. Red hearts O.

   K. Red and green hearts O.

   L. Berries P.

4. Tie a length of 40 wt. black cotton quilting thread to the center of the tag circle.

Cover Construction:

1. Pin the left side of the appliqué rectangle to one long side of the 7 3/4" x 10 1/2" red print rectangle with the right sides together and stitch using a **1/2"** seam allowance. Press the seam toward the red print. The cover should now measure 10 1/2" x 16 1/4".

2. Place the wrong side of the 10 1/2" x 16 1/4" flannel on the wrong side of the Step 1 unit. Machine baste around all edges using a scant 1/4" seam. Top stitch the cover 1/8" away from the seam on the red print side.

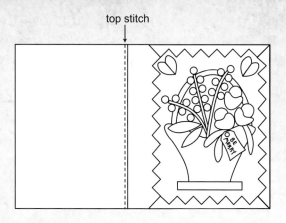

top stitch

3. Center an 8" length of twill tape on the right side of each short end of the cover and machine baste a scant 1/4" from end.

4. Finish one long side of each 3" x 10 1/2" side facing by turning under 1/4" **twice** and stitching 1/8" away from the edge. Finish one long side of each 1 1/2" x 13" top and bottom facing by turning under 1/4" **once** and stitching close to the edge.

5. Place each of the side facings on opposite ends of the cover, right sides together. Center the top and bottom facings across each long edge of the cover. Overlap the side facings approximately 7/8" then stitch 1/4" all the way around. Clip the corners. Turn right side out and press. Insert the cardboard cover of the composition book into the facings then close and tie the ribbons together in a bow.

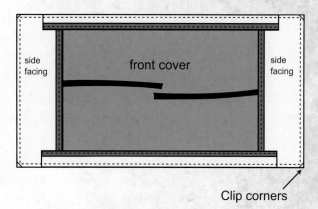

side facing

front cover

side facing

Clip corners

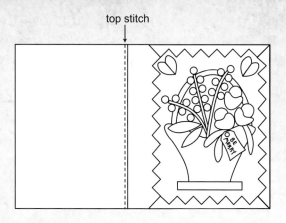

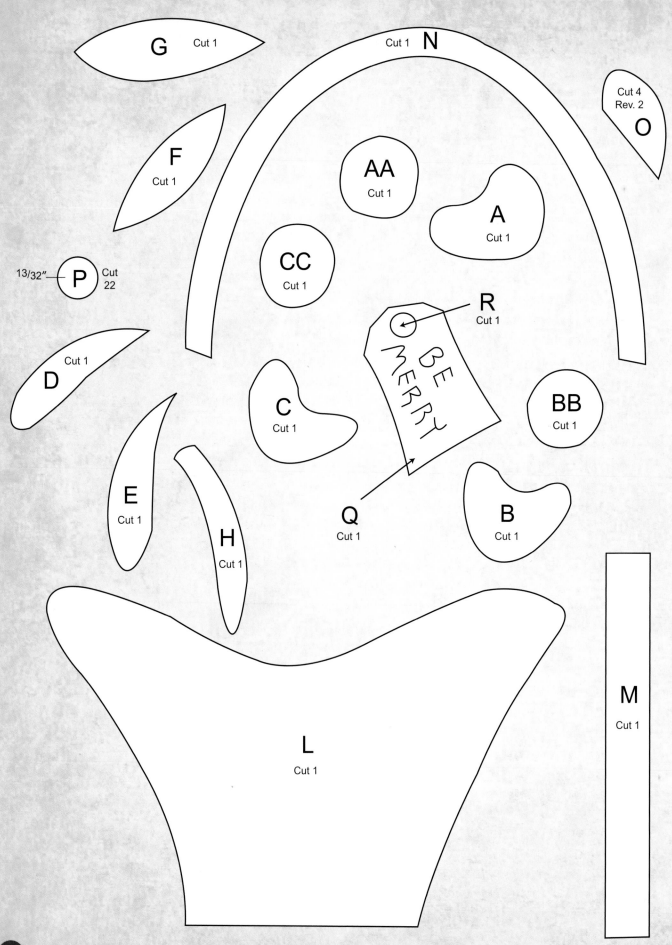

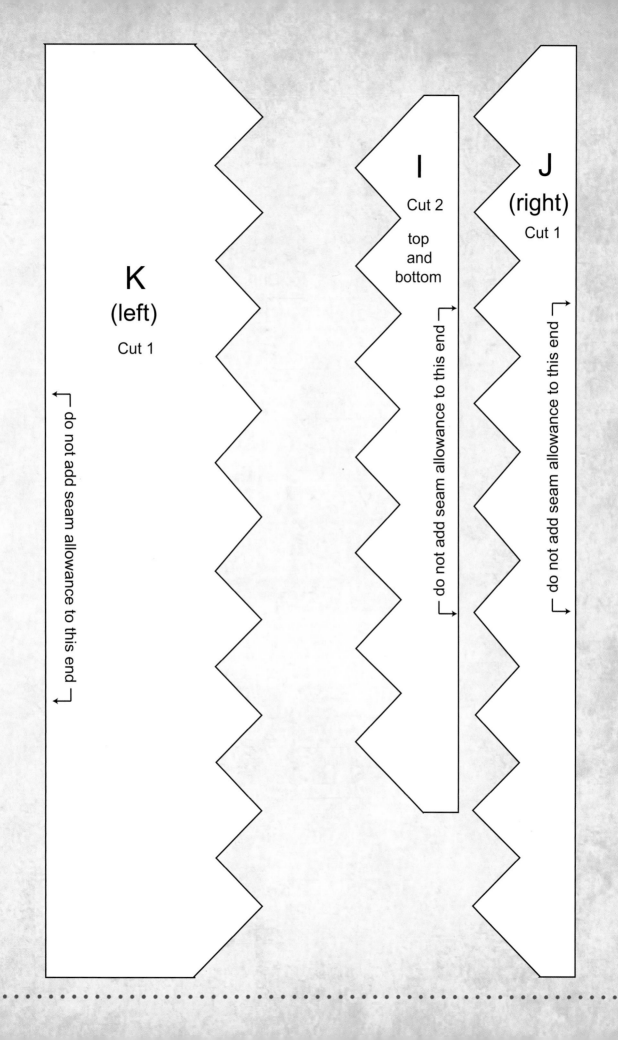

K
(left)

Cut 1

do not add seam allowance to this end

I
Cut 2

top
and
bottom

do not add seam allowance to this end

J
(right)
Cut 1

do not add seam allowance to this end

I will honour Christmas In my Heart

And try to Keep it All the year.
- Charles Dickens

Dickens Penny Rug was made by Martha Walker, Phoenix, Arizona.

Dickens Penny Rug

||||||||||||||||||||||||||||||||||||||||||||||||||||||

SIZE: 24" X 27"

A bouquet of heart-shaped blooms echo the sentiment proclaimed by Ebenezer Scrooge in Charles Dickens' 1843 classic, A Christmas Carol on this large wool appliqué table rug. The prairie cloth used as the appliqué foundation is a mid-weight cotton even weave fabric and can easily be cross stitched using waste canvas. Waste canvas is a temporary foundation for counted cross stitch. After the stitching is finished, the waste canvas threads are pulled out, leaving your stitches intact.

Fabric Requirements:

- ⊗ 2/3 yard light brown prairie cloth or homespun
- ⊗ 2/3 yard coordinating cotton print
- ⊗ 1/3 yard cranberry red plaid 1 wool felt
- ⊗ 12" square medium green wool felt
- ⊗ 4" square light green wool felt
- ⊗ 6" square medium green plaid wool felt
- ⊗ 6" square blue-green plaid wool felt
- ⊗ 1 fat eighth mahogany brown wool felt
- ⊗ 4" square cranberry red solid wool felt
- ⊗ 3" x 5" rectangle cranberry plaid 2 wool felt
- ⊗ 4" square light red houndstooth wool felt
- ⊗ 3" square gold wool felt

Other Supplies:

- ⊗ Aurifil Lana Wool Thread in the following colors:
  - ◊ 8951 - dark green
  - ◊ 8950 - medium green
  - ◊ 8140 - gold
  - ◊ 8089 - medium burgundy
  - ◊ 8465 - dark burgundy
- ⊗ 14 count waste canvas
- ⊗ #24 chenille needle

Cutting Instructions:

From light brown prairie cloth, cut:

- ⊗ 1 - 19" x 22" rectangle (appliqué background).

From coordinating cotton print, cut:

- ⊗ 1 - 19" x 22" rectangle (backing).

From cranberry red plaid wool felt, cut:

- ⊗ 26 - Tongues (template AA).
- ⊗ 26 - Tongues (template BB).

From mahogany brown plaid wool felt, cut:

- ⊗ 1 - Pot (template H).

From cranberry red solid wool felt, cut:

- ⊗ 1 - Pomegranate (template M).
- ⊗ 12 - Berries (template U).
- ⊗ 1 - Berry (template V).

From red plaid 2 wool felt, cut:

- ⊗ 1 - Pomegranate (template K).
- ⊗ 2 - Flowers (Reverse 1) (template S).

From light red houndstooth wool felt, cut:

- ⊗ 2 - Flowers (Reverse 1) (template T).
- ⊗ 3 - Flower centers (Reverse 1) (template P).

From gold wool felt, cut:

- ⊗ 3 - Flowers (Reverse 1) (template Q).
- ⊗ 2 - Flowers (Reverse 1) (template R).
- ⊗ 1 - Pomegranate (template N).

From medium green plaid wool felt, cut:

- ⊗ 1 - Holly leaf (template I).
- ⊗ 1 - Holly leaf (template J).
- ⊗ 1 - Pomegranate (template L).
- ⊗ 8 - Leaves (template A).

From medium green wool felt, cut:

- ⊗ 1 - 1/4" x 3 1/4" strip (pomegranate stem).
- ⊗ 1 - Leaf (template O).
- ⊗ 2 - Leaves (Reverse 1) (template E).
- ⊗ 2 - Leaves (Reverse 1) (template F).
- ⊗ 2 - Leaves (Reverse 1) (template G).
- ⊗ 14 - Leaves (Reverse 7) (template B).
- ⊗ 2 - 1/4" x 5 1/2" bias strips (Flower stems).
- ⊗ 2 - 1/4" x 6 1/2" bias strips (Flower stems).
- ⊗ 2 - 1/4" x 9" bias strips (Berry stems).

From light green wool felt, cut:

- ⊗ 16 - Leaves (Reverse 8) (template D).

From blue-green plaid wool felt, cut:

- ⊗ 2 - 1/4" x 6" bias strips (Flower stems).
- ⊗ 1 - 1/4" x 6 1/2" bias strip (Lower flower stem).
- ⊗ 10 - Leaves (template C).

Appliqué Shapes and Cross Stitch Lettering:

1. Unless otherwise indicated, use one strand of wool thread in a coordinating color and a blanket stitch to appliqué all shapes.

2. Transfer the design onto prairie cloth or homespun. Refer to the Appliqué Placement Diagram on page 59.

3. Appliqué Holly leaves I and J onto Pot H. Cover the ends of the holly leaves with Berry V to complete the pot unit.

4. Appliqué Pomegranate L onto Pomegranate M. Appliqué Pomegranate K to Pomegranate L/M unit to complete the pomegranate.

5. Baste the 1/4" x 3 1/4" medium green strip to the background for the pomegranate stem. Baste a 1/4" x 6" bias blue-green strip to opposite sides of the pomegranate stem where indicated. Baste the 1/4" x 5 1/2" medium green bias strips to opposite sides of the blue-green stems. Baste the 1/4" x 9" medium green bias strips for berry stems. Baste the 1/4" x 6 1/2" medium green bias strips for the lower flower stems. Appliqué all stems.

6. Appliqué the pot covering the stems using 3 strands of gold.

7. Appliqué the remaining shapes in the following order:

   A. Pomegranate O, Pomegranate N, Flowers R.

   B. Pomegranate K/L/M

   C. Flowers Q, S, and T.

   D. Flower centers P.

   E. Leaves A, B, C, D, E, F and G.

   F. Berries U.

8. Baste waste canvas over the cross stitch design areas where indicated on the diagram. Cross stitch the letters, using 3 strands of medium burgundy wool thread, stitching over 2 threads (for a 7 count per inch equivalent).

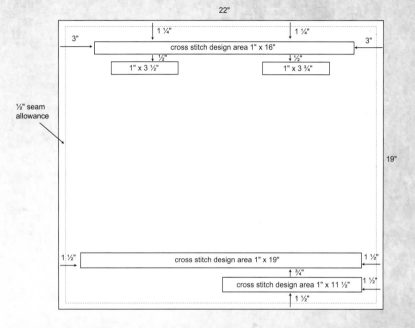

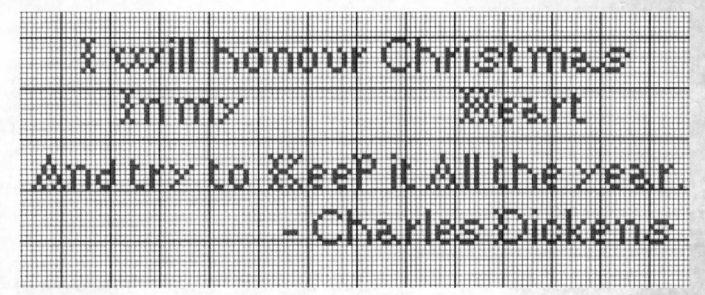

9. Appliqué the remaining blue-green stem, Flower Q and P and Leaves C as shown in bottom left corner.

10. Blanket stitch the outer edges of all Tongues AA and Tongues BB using 3 ply medium green wool thread.

Finish Rug:

1. Place 6 Tongues AA right sides together on each short side of rug top, beginning and ending 1/2" away from each edge. Machine baste using a 1/2" seam.

2. Place 7 Tongues AA right sides together on each long side of rug top, beginning and ending 1/2" away from each edge. Machine Baste using a 1/2" seam.

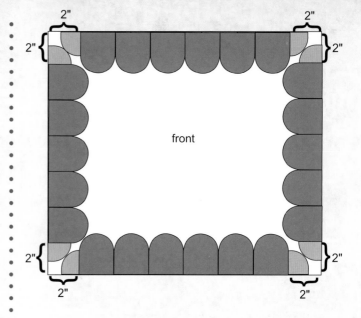

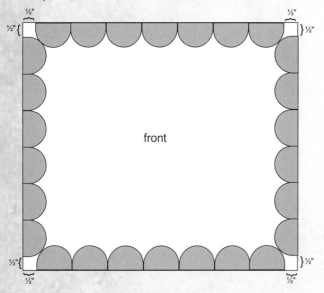

3. Place 5 tongues BB right sides together on each short side of rug top, beginning and ending 2" away from each edge. Stitch, using a 1/2" seam allowance.

4. Place six tongues BB right sides together on each long side of rug top, beginning and ending 2" away from each edge. Stitch, using a 1/2" seam allowance.

5. Turn the tongues right sides out. Press.

6. Referring to diagram, place a Tongue BB at each of the four corners by inserting the tongue in between the short and the long (top and bottom) tongues, and tack in place.

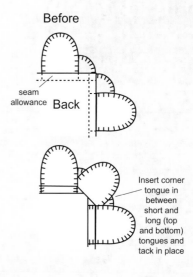

7. Blanket stitch the edge of the prairie cloth using 3 strands of medium burgundy wool thread.

8. Press under 1/2" on each edge of 19" x 22" backing and whipstitch to the back of the rug.

1"

I will honour Christmas
In my   Heart

And try to Keep it All the year.
– Charles Dickens

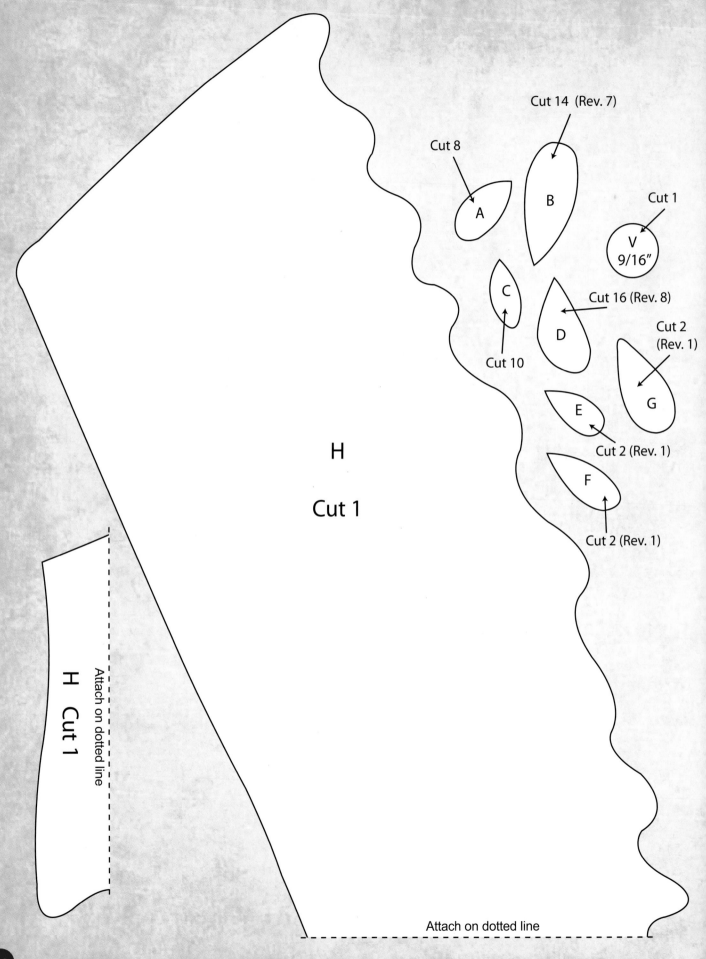

Cut 14 (Rev. 7)

Cut 8

Cut 1

A

B

V
9/16"

C

Cut 16 (Rev. 8)

D

Cut 2
(Rev. 1)

Cut 10

G

E

Cut 2 (Rev. 1)

H

Cut 1

F

Cut 2 (Rev. 1)

H Cut 1

Attach on dotted line

Attach on dotted line

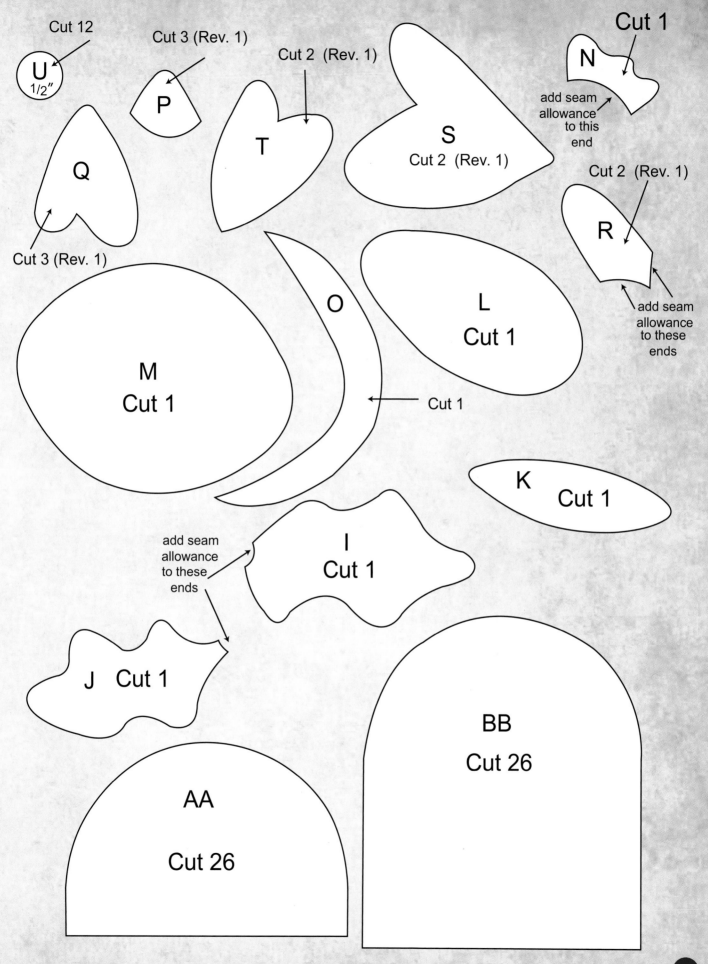

Cut 12

U 1/2"

Cut 3 (Rev. 1)

P

Cut 2 (Rev. 1)

T

Q

Cut 3 (Rev. 1)

Cut 1

N

add seam allowance to this end

S

Cut 2 (Rev. 1)

Cut 2 (Rev. 1)

R

add seam allowance to these ends

O

L Cut 1

M Cut 1

Cut 1

K Cut 1

add seam allowance to these ends

I Cut 1

J Cut 1

BB Cut 26

AA Cut 26

Blessings Penny Rug was made by Martha Walker, Phoenix, Arizona.

Blessings Penny Rug

||||||||||||||||||||||||||||||||||||||||||||||||||||||||||||||||||||||||||||||

SIZE: 10" X 14"

I was browsing through a book that had patriotic folk art images, and was looking at all of the wonderful images of eagles holding banners with "E Pluribus Unum" in their beaks. I decided to get out my sketchbook and sketch a different kind of bird, holding a banner with a different kind of message - and Blessings Penny Rug was the result.

Fabric Requirements:

- ⊗ 1 fat quarter black wool felt
- ⊗ 8" square red wool felt
- ⊗ 4" x 6" ivory wool felt
- ⊗ 4" x 5" red plaid wool felt
- ⊗ 2" x 4" light gold wool felt
- ⊗ 1" x 8" dark gold wool felt
- ⊗ 3" x 4" blue green wool felt
- ⊗ 1 fat quarter coordinating cotton fabric

Other Supplies:

- ⊗ Aurifil Lana Wool Thread in the following colors:
    - ◊ 8692 - black
    - ◊ 8323 - beige
    - ◊ 8951 - dark green
    - ◊ 8140 - gold
    - ◊ 8089 - medium burgundy
    - ◊ 8335 - brown
- ⊗ #24 chenille needle

Cutting Instructions:

From black wool felt, cut:

- ⊗ 1 - 8" x 12" rectangle.
- ⊗ 20 - Tongues (template A).

From coordinating cotton fabric, cut:

- ⊗ 1 - 9" x 13" rectangle.

From red wool felt, cut:

- ⊗ 20 - Tongues (template B).
- ⊗ 4 - Hearts (template C).
- ⊗ 6 - Berries (template D).

From ivory wool felt, cut:

- ⊗ 1 - Bird (template E).

From red plaid wool felt, cut:

- ⊗ 1 - Banner (template F).
- ⊗ 1 - Banner (template G).

From light gold wool felt, cut:

- ⊗ 1 - Wing (template H).

From dark gold wool felt, cut:

- ⊗ 1 - Branch (template I).
- ⊗ 1 - Branch (template J).

From blue-green wool felt, cut:

- ⊗ 1 - Leaf (template K).
- ⊗ 1 - Leaf (template L).
- ⊗ 1 - Leaf (template M).
- ⊗ 1 - Leaf (template N).
- ⊗ 1 - Leaf (template O).

Appliqué and Embroider Rug:

1. Embroider the lettering on banner F using 3 strands beige wool thread and a backstitch.

2. Embroider the x's on banner G using 3 strands beige wool thread and a long stitch.

3. Embroider the bird's eye using 2 strands black and a satin stitch.

4. Appliqué banner G to the black rectangle using 1 strand burgundy and a blanket stitch.

5. Appliqué the bird using 1 strand beige and a blanket stitch, leaving beak open.

6. Appliqué wing H to bird using 1 strand gold wool thread and a blanket stitch.

7. Insert banner F under bird's beak and complete bird. Appliqué banner F using 1 strand burgundy and a blanket stitch.

8. Appliqué branches I and J, tucking branch J under branch I. Whip stitch using 1 strand gold wool thread.

9. Embroider bird's legs using 2 strands gold and an outline stitch.

10. Appliqué leaves K, L, M, N, and O using 1 strand green wool thread and a blanket stitch. Embroider veins in leaves using 1 strand black wool thread and a back stitch.

11. Appliqué berries D using 1 strand burgundy and a whip stitch.

12. Appliqué hearts C using 1 strand black and a blanket stitch.

13. Appliqué tongues B onto each tongue A using 2 strands black and a blanket stitch.

14. Blanket stitch outside edges of each A/B tongue using 2 strands burgundy.

Finish Rug:

1. Place 4 tongues on each side of the rug and 6 tongues on the top and bottom. Overlap the tongues 1/2". Thread baste the tongues in place. Blanket stitch the edge of the rug to the tongues using 2 strands burgundy and a blanket stitch. Remove basting thread.

2. Press under 1/2" on all sides of backing rectangle. Whip stitch the backing to rug.

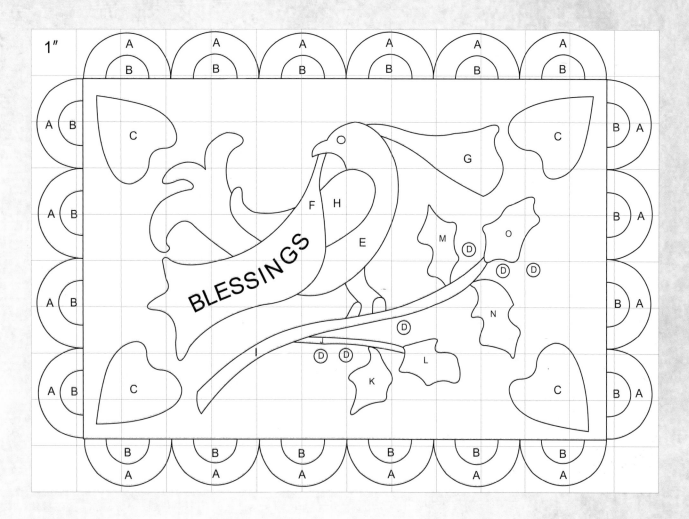

1"

BLESSINGS

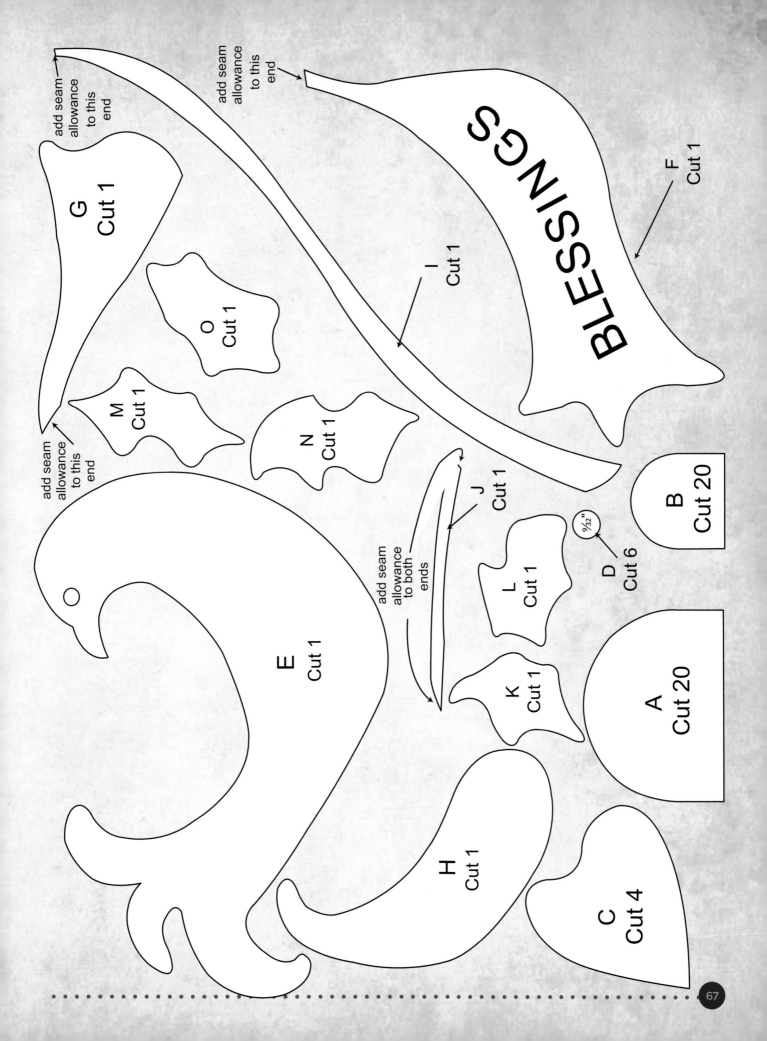

BLESSINGS

G
Cut 1

add seam
allowance
to this
end

add seam
allowance
to this
end

I
Cut 1

F
Cut 1

O
Cut 1

M
Cut 1

N
Cut 1

add seam
allowance
to this
end

J
Cut 1

B
Cut 20

E
Cut 1

add seam
allowance
to both
ends

L
Cut 1

9/32"
D
Cut 6

K
Cut 1

A
Cut 20

H
Cut 1

C
Cut 4

Dear Santa Album Cover was made by
Martha Walker, Phoenix, Arizona.

Dear Santa Album Cover

||||||||||||||||||||||||||||||||||||||||||||||||||||||||||||||||

FITS A STANDARD 8" X 8" SCRAPBOOK ALBUM
(WITH ACTUAL DIMENSIONS 9 3/4" X 8 5/8" AND A 1 1/8" SPINE)

With the popularity of scrapbooking today, the 8" x 8" scrapbook album is a staple in hobby stores. I designed this cover as a more homespun wrap for such an album. It's a great keepsake for those precious photographs of Christmases past or your children's letters to Santa (after he's read them, of course)!

Fabric Requirements:

- ⊗ 1/3 yard khaki prairie cloth
- ⊗ 6" square cranberry red wool felt
- ⊗ 6" square moss green wool felt
- ⊗ 6" square gold wool felt

Other Supplies:

- ⊗ Aurifil Lana Wool Thread in the following colors:
  - ◊ 8951 - Dark green
  - ◊ 8465 - Dark burgundy
- ⊗ 1 - 16" length of 1/2" ribbon
- ⊗ #24 chenille needle

Cutting Instructions:

From khaki prairie cloth, cut:

- ⊗ 1 - 10" x 22" rectangle (cover).
- ⊗ 2 - 3 3/8" x 10" strips (facings).

From gold wool felt, cut:

- ⊗ 4 - Large stars.
- ⊗ 4 - Small stars.

From moss green wool felt, cut:

- ⊗ 8 - 1/4" x 4" bias strips (main vine).
- ⊗ 12 - 1" x 3/16" bias strips (berry stems).
- ⊗ 18 – Leaves.

From cranberry red wool felt, cut:

- ⊗ "Dear Santa" letters.
- ⊗ 36 - 9/32" berries.

From ribbon, cut:

- ⊗ 2 - 8" lengths.

Appliqué Placement:

1. Transfer the design onto prairie cloth as shown.

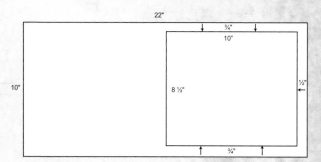

2. Prepare the appliqué shapes.

3. Appliqué the berry stems and main vine pieces onto the background with 1 strand of coordinating wool thread using a whipstitch.

4. Appliqué the stars and "Dear Santa" letters in place with 1 strand burgundy wool thread and a blanket stitch.

5. Appliqué the leaves and berries using 1 strand coordinating thread and a whip stitch.

Construct Cover:

1. Center an 8" length of ribbon on the right side of each short end of the cover and machine baste 1/4" from the end.

2. Finish one long side of each facing by turning under a 1/4" seam allowance twice and stitching.

3. Place each side facing right sides together on opposite ends of the cover. Stitch 1/2" away from the raw edges as shown. Clip corners. Turn right side out and press.

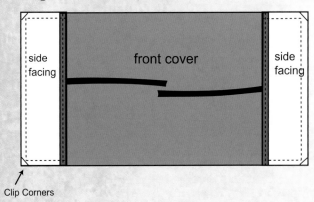

Clip Corners

4. Press under the remaining top and bottom edges of the cover 1/2". Top stitch close to the edge.

5. Insert the cover of the photo album into the facings, close and tie the ribbons together in a bow.

attach on dotted line

Holiday Hearts Hooked Rug was made by Martha Walker, Phoenix, Arizona.

Holiday Hearts Hooked Rug

||||||||||||||||||||||||||||||||||||||||||||||||||||||||||||||||||||||||||||||||

SIZE: 20" X 48"

A companion project to the Holiday Hearts Quilt, this rug could also be used as a table runner. The 100% wool I used for my strips came from a variety of sources. The primary red is wool that I found on the bolt and which I used as-is. The primary green started out as a sage green flannel off the bolt, which I over-dyed with Cushing Dyes for a rich leaf green. I even used a bit of recycled clothing, a camel-colored wool skirt I wore in the early 1980's, which I over-dyed as well. The rest of the wool was hand-dyed that I purchased at various quilt shops over time.

Fabric Requirements:

- ⊗ 1 yard monk's cloth, rug hooking linen, or Scottish burlap
- ⊗ 4 yards assorted golden beige wool
- ⊗ 2 yards red 1 wool
- ⊗ 1/2 yard assorted shades red wool
- ⊗ 1/2 yard leaf-green solid wool
- ⊗ 1 fat quarter dark green wool
- ⊗ 1/4 yard assorted greens

Other Supplies:

- ⊗ 4 1/2 yards 1" twill tape
- ⊗ 4 hanks (32 yards) red Persian wool yarn to match red 1 wool
- ⊗ Frame or hoop
- ⊗ Primitive hook
- ⊗ Wool cutter or rotary mat, rotary cutter and ruler
- ⊗ Wool cutter blades. The equivalent size in inches is parenthesized: size 6 (3/16"), size 8 (1/4"), size 9 (9/32").
- ⊗ Tapestry needle
- ⊗ Black Sharpie marker
- ⊗ Red Dot Tracer

Cutting Instructions:

1. Cut the backing fabric (monk's cloth, linen or burlap) 28" x 56" or larger.

2. Cut wool strips as needed in the width indicated. I recommend using a wool cutter for large projects such as this; however a rotary cutter or scissors may be used. Before cutting the strips, tear the wool fabric to find the straight of grain. Cut along the edge to start. Tear your piece again periodically to keep the strips on the straight of grain. (Strips will tear apart if they are on the bias.) When using a wool cutter, use fabric in manageable lengths of about 12".

3. Cut the solid leaf-green wool into #9 strips for flower stems.

4. Cut dark green wool into #6 strips for star outline.

5. Cut wool for remaining shapes into #8 strips.

Preparation:

1. Finish the edge of the backing with a zigzag stitch to prevent raveling.

2. Enlarge the rug design. Tape the Red Dot Tracing sheet over the design, aligning dots to

square up the corners. Trace over the design with a black Sharpie marker. Remove the Red Dot Tracer and pin or tape to the center of the rug backing fabric. Trace again over the design, pressing firmly so that the ink will penetrate through the tracing sheet onto the fabric.

3. Remove the Red Dot Tracer and retrace over any lines that may be hard to see. Be sure that the outside border lines and the lines within the "blocks" are aligned with the weave of the fabric.

General Hooking Directions:

1. Place the backing fabric on the frame or in a hoop, stretching the fabric taut.

2. With one hand, hold a wool strip underneath the backing. Insert the hook and pull up a "tail" (end of strip) at least one inch.

3. Push the hook into the next hole and pull up, pulling loop away from you so that it won't pull out the last loop or tail. The height of the loop should be the width of the strip or higher. When working with multiple widths, pick one height and stick with it!

4. Start the second strip in the same hole in which the previous tail ended. Hook into every second or third hole.

5. If possible, dovetail an adjoining row and hook the loops so they just touch the loops in the other row.

6. Hook just inside the outline of each shape, otherwise the shape will appear "fat". Hook the outline first and then fill in the shape.

7. Trim the ends even with the other loops after they are firmly surrounded by other hooking.

8. Push your finger into your rug. If it is hard to the touch, your loops are too close together.

Holiday Hearts Hooked Rug Hooking Directions:

1. Begin by hooking the border first. Hook two rows of red 1, followed by two rows of solid leaf green.

2. Outline the stars with #6 dark green strips. Fill with assorted greens.

3. Outline hearts with assorted reds. Fill each heart with a red which contrasts with its outline.

4. Hook stems with #9 solid leaf green strips.

5. Outline and fill the leaves with #8 solid leaf green strips.

6. Outline and fill the zigzag sashing with red 1.

7. Outline and fill the quadrant of each block using a different golden beige for each.

8. Outline and fill the remaining border with golden beige.

Finishing the Rug:

1. Press the rug using a hot iron. Place an almost dripping wet towel over the back of the rug and press down hard with your iron. Turn over rug, and lay the same towel over the front of the rug and press lightly. The rug will still be damp. Dry flat.

2. Fold the backing fabric to the back of the rug. Using 3 ply Persian wool yarn, whipstitch the edge using a tapestry needle.

3. Lay twill tape just over the yarn border and sew down, mitering the corners of the binding.

4. Cut the backing fabric away just inside the twill tape and sew the remaining edge of the binding to the rug.

1"

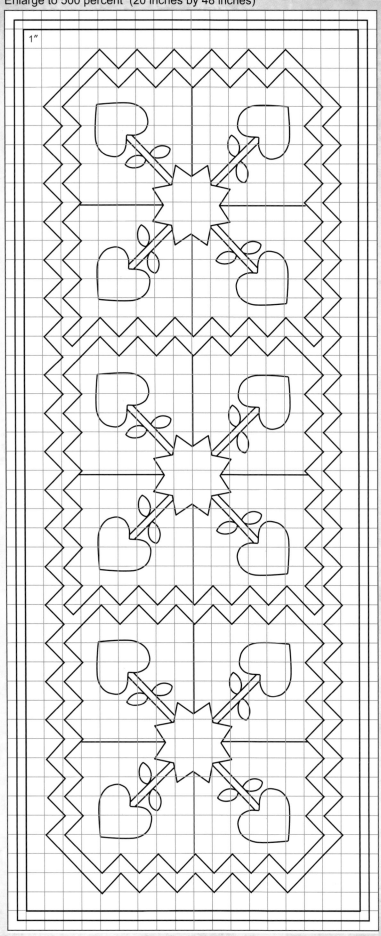

Enlarge to 500 percent (20 inches by 48 inches)

Centerpiece Punch Needle was made by Martha Walker, Phoenix, Arizona.

Centerpiece Punch Needle

SIZE: 3 1/4" X 3 1/4"

When I first saw a finished punch needle design in a needlework shop I was intrigued . . . it looked like a miniature hooked rug but was stitched using embroidery floss. It wasn't long before I had acquired the supplies to give it a try. I use a Cameo Ultra Punch needle that comes with detailed instructions on how to thread the needle and how to "punch" the design. Once you get started you'll be surprised at how easy and how fast it goes.

Supplies Needed:

- ⊗ Cameo Ultra Punch needle and threader
- ⊗ 10" square of weaver's cloth
- ⊗ Susan Bates embroidery hoop

⊗ Cotton Embroidery Floss:

◊ Background	tan	1219 Oak Weeks Dye Works 15 yards
◊ Vase	brown	1268 Molasses Weeks Dye Works 5 yards
◊ Stems and leaves	green	936 DMC
◊ Berries and border	red	814 DMC
◊ Flower	red	814 DMC
◊ Flower center	pink	3722 DMC
◊ Birds	tan	433 DMC
◊ Scallop dots	tan	3045 DMC
◊ Corner dots	red	814 DMC
◊ Bird eyes	dark brown	3371 DMC

Transfer the design onto the weaver's cloth. Place the cloth in a hoop, making sure it is drum tight.

Set your Cameo needle to #2 and thread with 3 strands of floss for each section. Begin by outlining the shape and then fill in the rest.

To finish the piece, trim the foundation cloth to 3/8" from the edge of the punched design. Fold to the back, leaving a 1/16" hem in front. Using 2 strands of DMC 3371 floss, sew a running stitch around the hem. Overcast the hem using 3 strands of color 3371. Be careful not to pull any of the loops from the punched design.

I tacked Centerpiece Punch Needle to cranberry red wool and mounted the wool onto foam core board for framing.

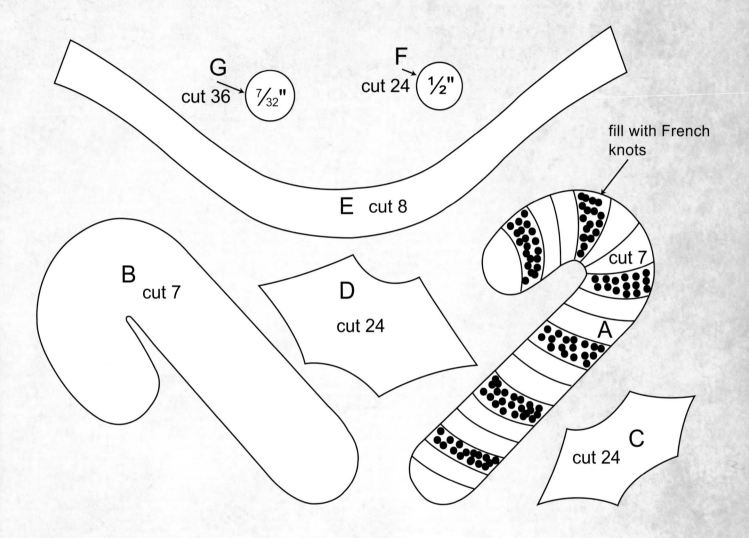

G cut 36 $^{7}\!/_{32}$"

F cut 24 ½"

fill with French knots

E cut 8

cut 7

B cut 7

D cut 24

A

C cut 24

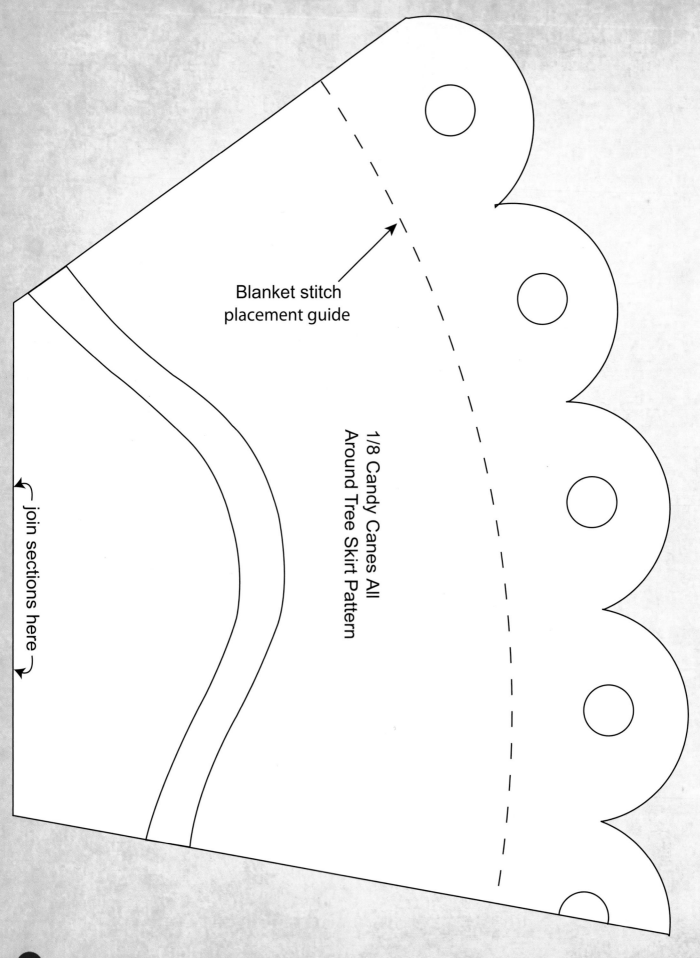

Blanket stitch
placement guide

1/8 Candy Canes All
Around Tree Skirt Pattern

join sections here

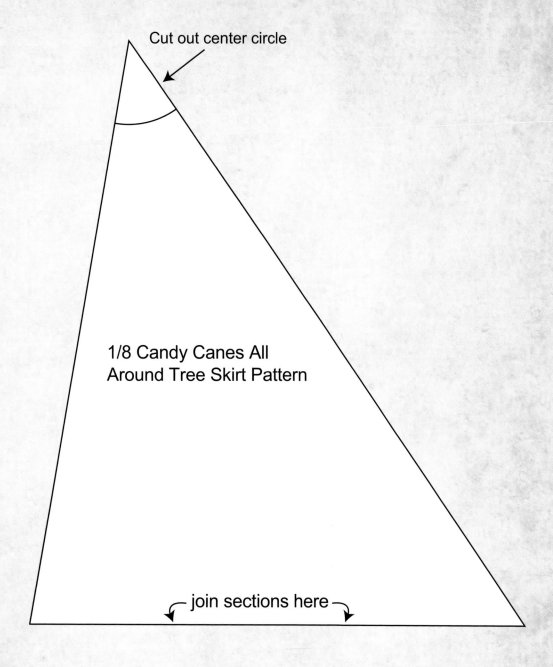

Cut out center circle

1/8 Candy Canes All
Around Tree Skirt Pattern

join sections here

Candy Cane Cornucopia Ornaments were made
by Martha Walker, Phoenix, Arizona.

Candy Cane Cornucopia Ornament

|||||||||||||||||||||||||||||||||||||||||||||||||||||||||||||||||||||||||||||||||||||||||||||||||||||||||

SIZE: 2 1/2" X 5"

The cornucopia ornaments during the Victorian era were made of paper and contained such things as tinsel and little cut out Christmas images. The Candy Cane Cornucopia is a more homespun rendition with a fabric cone trimmed in cotton chenille. The little postcard picks are miniaturized vintage postcard images with glittered edges. I have included a vintage Christmas postcard image from my collection for you to use. There is also clip art with similar imagery readily available from companies such as The Vintage Workshop.

Supplies needed:

- ⊗ 5" square piece fabric
- ⊗ 5" square piece craft-weight iron-on non-woven interfacing
- ⊗ Scrap medium green wool felt
- ⊗ Scrap light green wool felt
- ⊗ 1 1/2 yards Crystal Palace maroon chenille yarn
- ⊗ 3 maroon 6mm round glass beads (Darice)
- ⊗ Maroon thread
- ⊗ 20 gauge tarnish resistant craft wire (gold)
- ⊗ Tacky glue
- ⊗ Paper clay
- ⊗ Awl
- ⊗ Wire cutters
- ⊗ Acrylic paint - lt. ivory, maroon
- ⊗ Delta Instant Age Varnish
- ⊗ Decorative edge scissors (sm. Victorian)
- ⊗ 1/8" diameter wood dowel
- ⊗ White glitter
- ⊗ Vintage postcard image
- ⊗ White cardstock
- ⊗ Parchment colored crinkle paper
- ⊗ Polyester fiberfill

Cornucopia:

1. Trace and cut out the cone onto non-shiny side of craft-weight interfacing with a pencil. Mark the fold line and dots for the handle. Fuse to the wrong side of the fabric following the manufacturer's directions. Cut out the fabric following the interfacing edge.

2. Fold tab along the fold line and spread tacky glue along the tab. Shape the cone and glue the tab to the inside of the cone, matching the top edge. Work your way down to the end of the cone.

3. Use the awl to pierce holes for the handles where marked.

4. Cut 6" of wire and insert the ends through the holes to make a handle. Fold the ends up 1/4" to secure the handle. Trim the excess wire with wire cutters.

5. Wrap the wire with a 16" length of chenille yarn. Tie a knot around one end of the handle, then begin wrapping the wire, putting a small bead of tacky glue on the wire an inch at a time.

6. Cut 3 pieces of yarn into 9" lengths. Knot the ends together. Glue the knot at the seam on the cone's edge. Put a bead of tacky glue an inch at a time along the edge and glue the yarn along the edge, twisting the 3 strands together as you

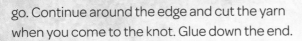

go. Continue around the edge and cut the yarn when you come to the knot. Glue down the end.

7. Cut 1 leaf pattern B from medium green felt and 2 leaf patterns C from light green felt.

8. Using maroon thread and a running stitch, sew each light green leaf onto both sides of pattern B. Tack 3 maroon beads to the center of the holly leaves and tack to the outside of the cone below the handle.

Postcard Pick:

1. Color copy a vintage postcard onto ivory cardstock to a size approximately 1 3/8" x 2 1/8". Cut out 1/4" beyond image. Cut a piece of plain cardstock 1 7/8" x 2 5/8" and glue to back of the postcard around the top and sides. Leave the bottom end open.

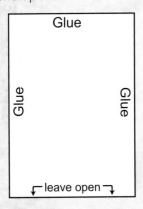

2. When dry, cut around the image using decorative edge scissors.

3. Cut a 2 1/4" length of wood dowel. Dip one end of the dowel in tacky glue and insert into the open end of the card and press together. Dab glue around the edges of the postcard and shake glitter onto the glue.

Candy Canes:

1. Roll paper clay into 3/16" thick rolls and shape into candy canes about 3 1/4" long. Let dry then paint with one coat of light ivory. Paint the stripes in maroon. Varnish with 1 coat of Instant-age varnish.

Insert a small bit of fiberfill in the bottom of the cone. Top with a small amount of crinkle paper. Insert the postcard pick and candy canes.

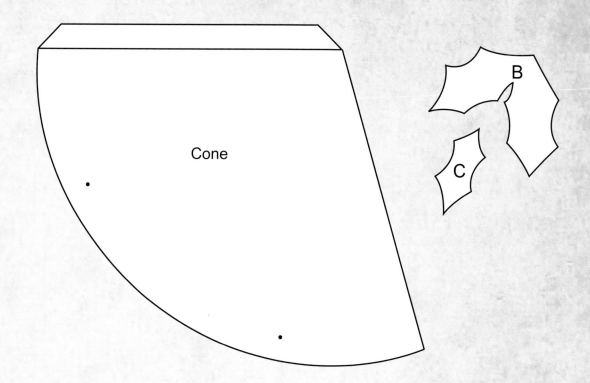

Cone

B

C

Holly Tree Top Star was made by
Martha Walker, Phoenix, Arizona.

Holly Tree Top Star

||||||||||||||||||||||||||||||||||||||||||||||||||||||||||||||||||||||||||||||||

SIZE: 4" PLUS WIRE WRAP

Supplies:

⊗ 5" square antique white wool

⊗ 5" square cotton coordinating fabric

⊗ 2" square medium green wool felt and embroidery floss to match

⊗ 2" square light green wool felt

⊗ Craft-weight iron-on non-woven interfacing

⊗ 18" maroon chenille trim

⊗ Maroon embroidery floss

⊗ 3 - red 6mm round glass glitter beads (Darice)

⊗ 30" - 19 gauge craft wire (Darice)

⊗ Wire cutters

⊗ Tacky glue

⊗ Drill and 1/16" drill bit

⊗ 3 1/2" precut wooden star, 1/8" thick (Darice)

Instructions:

1. Wrap wire over a bottle neck to form a cone shape. Straighten 1" of the wire at top.

2. Drill a hole in the star 1/4" deep with the 1/16" drill bit.

Wood star

Drill hole 1/4" deep

3. Use the wooden star as your template to trace 2 stars onto the dull side of the interfacing. Cut out the interfacing stars without adding a seam allowance.

4. Press one interfacing star to the wool and cut close to the interfacing.

5. Press the remaining interfacing star to the wrong side of the coordinating cotton and cut out with a 3/8" seam allowance around the interfacing. Clip the seam allowance at the angles. Set aside.

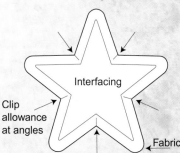

Interfacing on fabric

Interfacing

Clip allowance at angles

Fabric

6. Cut 5 holly leaves using template A from medium green felt and 5 holly leaves using template B from the light green felt. Place each light green leaf B in the center of a medium green leaf A and secure with 3 running stitches using 1 strand of maroon embroidery floss.

7. Whipstitch the leaves to the center of the wool star as shown using 1 strand of green embroidery floss.

8. Sew 3 beads to the center of the leaves.

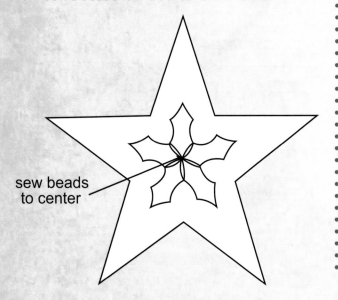

sew beads to center

9. Glue the interfacing side of the fabric star to one side of the wooden star with tacky glue. Fold the seam allowance over the edge of the star and glue to back of the wood.

10. Glue the interfacing side of the wool star to the other side of the wooden star. Glue the wire into the drilled hole in the wooden star. Glue chenille trim to the outside of the star edge.

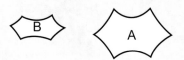

Sparrow Clips were made by
Martha Walker, Phoenix, Arizona.

Sparrow Clips

SIZE: 2" X 5"

For each bird you will need:

- ⊗ 8" x 10" rectangle brown small print fabric and thread to match
- ⊗ 2 black "E" beads
- ⊗ Black quilting thread
- ⊗ Polyester fiberfill
- ⊗ 1 - 13/4" clothespin
- ⊗ Walnut stain
- ⊗ Acrylic brush
- ⊗ Tacky glue

Instructions:

1. Cut 2 - 2 1/2" x 6" rectangles from brown print. Trace the bird body onto the wrong side of one rectangle, marking A, B, C and D. This tracing line will be the sewing line.

2. Place the rectangle with the bird tracing on top of the second rectangle with right sides together. Using a very small stitch length, stitch on the drawn line, leaving the seam open between A and B, and C and D. Trim the seam allowance to 3/16", except between A and D, leave a 1/4" seam allowance. Clip the seam at A and B. Clip the curves.

3. Trace the bird underside onto the wrong side of the brown print. Mark points A and B. Add a 1/4" seam allowance and cut out on this line.

4. With right sides together, sew the underside to the bird body from A to B, leaving open on one side where indicated. Turn right side out. A loop turner works well for turning the tail section.

5. Whipstitch the tail closed between C and D. Lightly stuff the tail.

6. Topstitch lines on the tail using a long stitch length.

7. Stuff the remainder of the bird. Whipstitch the opening closed between A and B.

8. Sew black "E" beads on both side of the bird where indicated using black quilting thread.

9. Stain the clothespin with walnut stain. Glue the underside of the bird to the clothespin using tacky glue.

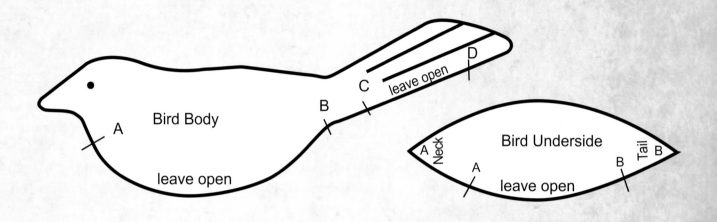

Bird Body

A

leave open

B

C   leave open

D

Bird Underside

A   Neck

A

leave open

B   Tail   B

About the Author

Martha Walker began making quilts as a teenager in the early 1970's. Since then she has gravitated toward traditional textile arts such as embroidery, rug hooking, wool appliqué, and her first love, quilt making.

In her efforts to challenge herself both artistically and technically, Martha began exhibiting her original designs in national and international quilt shows in 1994. She has won numerous awards including ribbons at International Quilt Festival (2005), American Quilter's Society Quilt Show (2000, 2007), National Quilter's Association Quilt Show (2005), Pacific International Quilt Festival (2006), Road to California (2001, 2002), Mid-Atlantic Quilt Festival (2002), and The Arizona Quilter's Guild Quilt Show (1996, 1999, 2001, 2003, 2005, and 2007).

Martha publishes patterns through her company, Wagons West Designs and recently authored the book *Vintage Christmas*.

Martha is married with two sons, Nicholas and Andrew, and daughter-in-law, Katie. She lives with her husband, Thom, and Nicholas in Phoenix, Arizona.

Acknowledgements

In 1980, I was back in Kansas City after graduating from college. Armed with a pair of scissors, I eagerly clipped any and all quilt patterns I found published in The Kansas City Star. The newspaper occasionally ran a feature called, "More Old Favorites from The Star," reprints of the old quilting patterns from the 20s, 30s, 40s and 50s. I later inherited some of my grandmother's Star patterns she herself had clipped out in the 1930's.

I am extremely grateful to Doug Weaver and Diane McClendon for giving me the opportunity to work with a company that has played such an important role in the history of quilting and in my own history as well.

My sincere thanks go to my editor, Edie McGinnis, for her thoughtful advice and guidance from beginning to end. I appreciated her valuable suggestions and her playful sense of humor while getting the job done.

Photography is such an important element in a quilt book and my thanks go to Aaron Leimkuehler for his wonderful work. It was a fun day at the photo shoot!

Thanks to Lon Eric Craven for doing such a wonderful job on the illustrations that add so much to the book.

Kelly Ludwig is the designer who made the cover and pages look so lovely. Thank you, Kelly!

Thanks to all of my quilting friends and colleagues who have provided camaraderie and support in my quilting endeavors over the years.

And thank you to my husband, Thom, who supports me in countless ways and went out of his way to accommodate the time I spent making this book a reality!